Listening to Butterflies

For Erin

With thanks for your generous
support & company in our
editing workshop, Aspen 2019.
Good luck with your
book, & please let me know when
it gets published.
Julian.

Listening to Butterflies

IN SEARCH OF MAN'S RELATIONSHIP WITH NATURE

BY JULIAN D. NIHILL

MALAIKA BOOKS

ISBN: 0692407227
ISBN 13: 9780692407226

"If industrial man continues to multiply his numbers and expand his operations he will succeed in his apparent intention, to seal himself off from the natural and isolate himself within a synthetic prison of his own making. He will make himself an exile from the earth and then will know, at last, if he is still capable of feeling anything, the pain and agony of final loss."
Edward Abbey: *Desert Solitaire.* 1968

———

"Modern Man talks of a battle with Nature,
forgetting that if he won the battle,
he would find himself on the losing side."
E.F. Schumacher: *Small is Beautiful: a study of economics
as if people mattered.* 1973

TABLE OF CONTENTS

Map of Kenya and Tanganyika · xi

Chapter 1   La Flor de Asfalto · 1

Chapter 2   The Sun Sets on Kenya's Happy Valley · · · · · · · · · · · · · · 15

Chapter 3   The Chief Justice, the President, and the Mau Mau · · · · · · 27

Chapter 4   Childhood in the Haven of Peace · · · · · · · · · · · · · · · · 46

Chapter 5   Of Schoolboys and Other Animals · · · · · · · · · · · · · · · 69

Chapter 6   The Colonial Identity · 83

Chapter 7   Massacre and Revolution · 89

Chapter 8   Roman Catholics, Russian Orthodox, and Humanists · · · · 103

Chapter 9   Travels in the Levant · 120

Chapter 10 Discovering Kenya · 131

Chapter 11 Cairo to Nairobi Overland · · · · · · · · · · · · · · · · · · · 149

Chapter 12 Rivers of Blood · 158

Chapter 13 America · 166

Chapter 14 Outward Bound in Mexico · · · · · · · · · · · · · · · · · · · 176

Chapter 15 Kilimanjaro and Sokoke · 181

Chapter 16 Sahara: The Inward Journey · · · · · · · · · · · · · · · · · · · 197

Chapter 17 Dialogues in the Desert · 220

Chapter 18 A Fable · 234

MAP OF KENYA AND TANGANYIKA

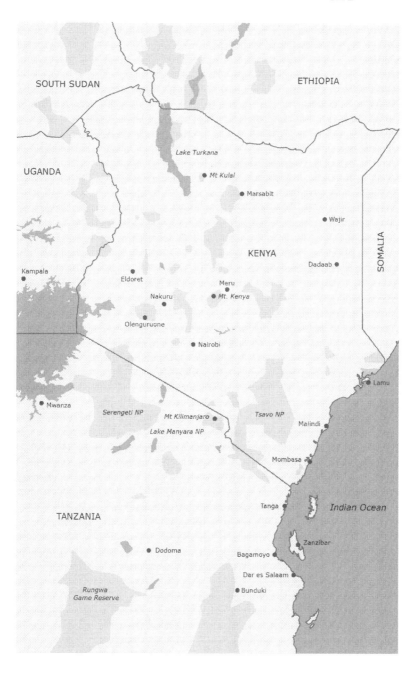

CHAPTER 1

La Flor De Asfalto

2010

It all started with a snatch of verse from Paul Verlaine.

We had met at a dinner where I was a last minute addition to make up the numbers. Our conversation was polite, trivial and almost completely in Spanish. "I am tax lawyer, a U.S. tax lawyer", I told her.

"And I a literature professor. Why do you live in Mexico if you are a _U.S._ tax lawyer?"

"Well, partially because of the niche of tax law that I am in, but really more because I started a Foundation here which takes a lot of my time." I immediately regretted opening that subject. Outward Bound is complicated to explain, and my general experience with new acquaintances is that they become uncomfortable with the discussion. People don't like to get into heavy topics when they first meet. Too many shoals in those waters. When she dutifully followed up, I dodged to another subject.

"So what do you do with your time when you are not lawyering or working on your Foundation? Of course, assuming you do have interests other than your work. So many _norteamericanos_ seem to be monofocal when it comes to work."

Once again, the dilemma. Do I correct her and tell her that I am not an American, that I was born of Irish and French parents in Kenya, and lived in East Africa through my formative years? That while I had lived many years in America, I did not consider myself a "norteamericano"? Leaving the initial impression alone for the moment I responded, "Monofocal and monolingual, no doubt," suggesting that the barb was inappropriate. The Mexicans have a thing about Americans only speaking one language. Overused joke: *"What do you call a person who speaks three languages?" "Trilingual". "What do you call a person who speaks two languages?" "Bilingual". "What do you call a person who speaks only one language?" "Monolingual." "No, an American."*

"Actually, I have taken up biking. It's a new interest for me since I came to Mexico."

Switching to English, for no apparent reason, Angelica cheerfully responded, "Oh I do too. I always ride around my bicycle in the city."

No need to comment on the grammar, I thought, my Spanish is far from perfect. "I live near the Desierto de los Leones, and there are hundreds of excellent, challenging trails for mountain bikers. We should go together someday."

We were not in synch. We had completely different visions of biking. Angelica is a self-confessed *"flor de asfalto"*, a flower that grows in the cracks of a city sidewalk. She is completely urban. Her interests are literature, music, theatre, and architecture. A bicycle is a utilitarian tool for getting around in a city where traffic impedes the flow of arteries worse than uncooked steak. She shrugged off the disconnect. "How do you find living in our city of 26 million people?"

"I find it fascinating. So many layers of culture, of civilization. But, I fear I am only scratching the surface."

Toward the end of the dinner we talked about the architecture of Mexico City and she offered to show me her city, by bicycle of course. Accepting her invitation I said, "I'd love to see the city through the eyes of someone who is so steeped in its history and culture."

So later that month we found a Sunday when we could bike the city. We rode from the hotel zone past the Tamayo and The Modern Art museums, across to Chapultepec Park, to the Avenida de las Poetas, a path through the Park dotted with busts of great poets.

"Is Poetas feminine?" I asked, noting that it ends in *a*, the feminine ending. "Because I am not seeing any women poets here."

"No, it is one of those words that come from Greek, like problema, paradigma, sistema, enigma, which are masculine and end in a. But, the disappointing thing is how we Mexicans give so little credit to our women poets. Here is an avenue dedicated to Mexican poets, Avenida de las Poetas, and not one woman. Don't think we don't have any. Sor Juana, Rosario Castellanos, Elena Poniatowska. You know, if you look around this city, which has literally hundreds of statues of famous people, you can count on one hand, and excluding the thumb, how many statues there are of women. I don't mean statues of symbolic women, like Motherhood, or Grace. I mean women who were flesh and blood. One of the few is the Diana, the famous statue of the naked huntress in the middle of Reforma. It was modelled after Helvia Martinez Verdayes, reputed to be the mistress of the President, and later married to one of the country's most corrupt men, the head of Pemex. She posed nude for the work at 16 years old."

"Aha. The age-old Latin woman's dilemma, no doubt. *Ama de casa* (housewife) or *amante.*"

We crossed over to La Condesa, one of Mexico City's early residential neighbourhoods, where Angelica showed me the Edificio Basurto with its elegant circular staircase, the oval Calle Amsterdam, originally a horse racetrack, now ringed by its Art Deco and Art Nouveau homes. Initially, I was ill at ease with the torrent of vehicles even as Angelica negotiated the traffic with ease. "Does anyone stop for lights or pedestrians or even, God forbid, cyclists?" I asked, after a close call with a cab driver who cut in front of me. "Don't worry, they never actually hit the bikers," she replied carelessly, though she was concerned that her "American" friend would not be able to cope with the city. From there, on to the great fountains of Cibeles and then Parque Mexico, where Rastafarian drummers gathered to play their djembes, and the steps and curves around the plaza offered great opportunities for a more free form cycling. Responding to the drummers and the general laid back atmosphere, I started to have fun, to jump sidewalks, to bounce down steps, to free wheel a bit. Later she admitted that it was not until this moment that she began to think: "Maybe he is not so uptight and gringo."

After that ride we decided to walk to a small bistro in the heart of the restaurant district near her home. There is a broad, almost Parisian avenue called Horacio, in the Polanco neighbourhood. Its layout is similar to that of a Parisian arrondissement, with its boulevards and diagonal streets named after Lamartine, Voltaire, and Victor Hugo. As we walked down the *camellon,* a central walking path between the two lanes of traffic, it started to rain. Not a hard rain, but a drizzle – what the Irish call a "soft rain" – the kind that makes you want to curl up with a book as the skies lose their luminescence and turn grey, the kind that leads to introspection and moroseness. In the cold and wet I offered to share my jacket. We nudged closer. Out of nowhere there came to me a snippet of verse, which I recited quietly, almost to myself:

Il pleure dans mon coeur comme il pleut sur la ville.[a]

And, without missing a beat, Angelica continued:

Quelle est cette langeur qui penètre mon couer?[b]

We looked at each other thinking: "Did you just say that? Where did that come from?" Neither of us expected that connection. Angelica's husband had recently left her, and with my divorce under way, we both understood *"cette langeur qui penètre mon couer."* It was not just the shared emotion, albeit fleeting, of recognising that there was something missing, a sense of melancholy in each of our souls. It was the startling recognition that the stereotypes we had in mind were keeping us from seeing each other completely and that there were layers to these onions.

After that, Angelica opened her world to me a crack. She invited me to an evening reading group she led twice a month. My first evening, we discussed Paul Auster's *New York Trilogy*. I had never heard of "post modernism." Post modern writing. Postmodern architecture. Post modern this and post modern that. Everyone else in the group seemed to be completely at ease with this terminology. Paul Auster is "post modern" explained one of the group members

---

a Tears fall in my heart, as it rains in the city.
b What is this languor that pierces my heart.

"because he writes about the complex absurdity of contemporary life, about moral and philosophical relativism." I wondered what was modern if this was post modern, and what would come next. Post post-modern? "Don't worry about tags and labels," Angelica told me, "try to enjoy the abstractness, the sense that Auster wants you to be part of the story, as though you are inside a detective novel." In *Ghosts,* the second story in the trilogy, I was surprised, and delighted, to find Auster writing about Thoreau and his experience living alone in a cabin in the woods for two years more than a hundred years ago. With Edward Abbey, and Walt Whitman, Thoreau is one of my favourite writers. In *Ghosts* Auster writes, I believe autobiographically, about a writer named Fanshawe, who escapes to live like Thoreau, and who finds that "Solitude became a passageway into the self, an instrument of discovery," and that "from now on [his] work is no longer promising — it is fulfilled, accomplished, unmistakably his own."

After class I invited Angelica to join me for what I dubbed "a Walden weekend," to explore this idea of solitude as an instrument of discovery. We camped in the caldera of the volcano of the Nevado de Toluca. After a cold, and rather restless night, we set out early for the rim of the volcano, some 15,000 feet above sea level. I told her: "Try not to look up. Don't wonder how far there is to go. Take small paces, one foot just in front of the other. Get yourself into a Zen mode in which you think of nothing but the footstep ahead of you." And so we climbed for a couple of hours, mostly in silence. As we approached the rim, I took her hand and asked her to keep her eyes down for the last twenty metres. We reached the rim and the view east and west unfolded toward eternity. I told her she could break her Zen trance and look up. Raising her head and looking around, tears welled in her eyes and gradually over-flowing, streamed down her cheeks. This *flor de asfalto* had never witnessed such dramatic beauty in Nature. We saw Popocateptl and Iztlazihuatl, both snow-capped volcanoes, rising over 17,000 feet into the cold, clear air, some hundred miles to the east, across the cruel harshness of one of the largest cities in the world, Mexico City. We gazed west toward the Pacific, over the hills of Valle de Bravo where I owned a plot of land. We looked back into the lake beside which we had slept, deep in the caldera of this extinct volcano. We were alone with the wind and our thoughts.

A few days later, we took turns reading the next chapters of *Ghosts* aloud. In my turn we came to the passage where Blue, a key character *"comes across a sentence"*, I intoned, *"that finally says something to him — Books must be read as deliberately and reservedly as they were written — and suddenly he understands that the trick is to go slowly...What he does not know is that if he were to find the patience to read the book in the spirit in which it asks to be read, his entire life would begin to change."*

"Stop there," Angelica interrupted. "Auster is saying the same thing here, with Blue, that he was saying with Fanshawe and Thoreau. Fanshawe is so wrapped up in his urban world that he needs to escape to a quiet place where he can absorb a different rhythm, like we did on the Nevado. Blue is like you, always active, restless, not reflective. Books, the great books especially, are like Nature. They ask you to not just accept them, not just glance over them, or skate through them. They ask you to immerse yourself in them. And by immerse yourself, I don't just mean spending time with them. I mean plunging in, as you would if you were scuba diving, cut off from the world we know, where time and space change, and the sound of your breath sets the rhythm at which you perceive the world." She was right. Although I read a lot, I had a tendency to "skate through" the books I read. I resolved to slow down, to read "deliberately". "Interesting," I thought, "Thoreau used the same word – deliberately - when he decided to go to the woods to live."

Later we discussed Julian Barnes, *The History of the World in 10 ½ Chapters*. Although he is a Brit, and my *tocayo*,[c] I had not read anything by him. We were both struck by how subtly Barnes introduces the theme of Man creating rules about the Divine, rules that govern our conduct: from the trial and excommunication of the woodworm, based, we discovered, on the true trials of animals in the Middle Ages;[d] to the search for Noah's ark on Mount Ararat; to the wonderful last ½ chapter in which the narrator dies, goes to Heaven and discovers that he can have whatever he wants… countless games of golf in which his score keeps getting lower until he completes the 18 hole course in 18 shots; where he has endless sex with gorgeous women, night after night; where his football team always wins. He ultimately asks his companion, a kind of chaperone from this Heaven: "but, where is God?" She responds "God? Do you want God? Is that what you want?" And, after they discuss that God is optional in this Heaven, he asks what sort of Heaven people usually want. She replies: "They want a continuation of life. But… better, needless to say." He asks, "Sex, golf, shopping, dinner, meeting famous people and not feeling bad?" Angelica and I mused over how different is the vision different cultures create for their Heaven, based on their own society.

---

c Spanish for namesake, but only referring to the first, or Christian, name. Often Mexicans with the same first name refer to each other affectionately as "tocayo".

d E.P. Evans: *The Criminal Prosecution and Capital Punishment of Animals.*

I invited Angelica to sail with me in the Sea of Cortez. Thirty years earlier, on an elegant pleasure yacht in the same sea, a client, DK, had initiated me to his mantra: He who dies with the most toys wins. When I returned to Baja with Angelica, I thought of DK and of Julian Barnes. We rented a chunky, twenty-two foot, cabin cruiser, with just enough room for the two of us to sleep in different nooks below deck. No engine. No cabin lights. No waiters. No one to fetch or pick up things for us. Just ourselves. This boat was far from being a Toy, but it served its purpose, which was to enjoy the beauty of this remarkable stretch of coastline. We sailed to Isla Dansante, not far from Puerto Escondido, and anchored in a bay protected on three sides from wind and tides. That afternoon we kayaked for a couple of hours. Spotting a school of dolphins playing by a point, we paddled toward them. Two broke from the school and came to investigate us. They approached from the front, seeking us out inquisitively, undulating in and out of the waves, playing in the surf, taking deep breaths as they dove, and then blowing out from their blowholes as they surfaced. We were enchanted by the sound of the exhale, the curve of their sleek, black bodies as they ducked below our paddles, the excitement of the moments when they broke dramatically from the sea and appeared to dance on their flukes.

The opening to the bay lay to the west of our anchorage. To the north, east and south, was volcanic rock, resting like the hump of a whale, dark against the sky. That night, as the sun sank in the west, shafts of light darted across the waves entering the bay, and set a glow on the rocky slopes of the eastern shore, deep orange, almost red, as they reflected the setting sun. Then all was dark. The wind died too, and with the darkness, came stillness. There was barely a ripple, other than the gentle swell of a dying wave as it glided across the bay. We lay on the cockpit benches, looking up at the sky. Black. Black without a star in sight. And the moon was not due to rise for several hours.

Angelica challenged me, "I bet I see the first star before you."

Sounding more knowledgeable than I was, I responded, "It will be Venus, the brightest star, and it will rise just above the saddle of the hill to our east."

As we lay there, peering into the darkness, stars began to appear. At first like dim headlamps from a distant pilgrim, solitary, soft, faint. Then, another, and another, suddenly accelerating in their appearance, until within ten minutes the sky was littered with lights, shining, twinkling, linking up with each other, all across the bowl of night. But it did not stop with the sky. The sea, so calm, became a mirror, reflecting each star without a blur, a phosphorescent meadow.

Then the magic happened. We heard the sound of two dolphins breaching and blowing. I might have missed them if Angelica had not asked: "What is that?" Unmistakably two dolphins, swimming together, close to our boat. We could not see them. We only heard them. But in the darkness and the calm, we felt we could touch them. We were part of their world. Silent spectators, not voyeurs or intruders, because we felt welcomed, a part of the natural moment. We wondered if it was the same pair of dolphins that had played with us that afternoon. "They don't care that we're here," said Angelica. "They accept us." For her, animals had been alien, threatening creatures. Now she felt we were part of their world and they meant us no harm.

Through Angelica's wonder, I started to see the natural world the way I had seen it 40 years before. I remembered the nights in Tsavo when travelling around Kenya as a young man we heard elephants grazing as they passed by our tent. I remembered being aware that our presence did not bother them, and I felt the same sense of being "at one" with the dolphins as I had felt four decades before with the elephants. I had forgotten the feeling of being immersed in Nature and that so long as I agreed to be part of that world, did not to try to dominate it, re-arrange it, beat it back to where it did not impinge on me, I was safe within it.

———

Verlaine may have been the catalyst, but it was Karen Blixen who cemented our relationship. One evening Angelica asked me to describe our home in Kenya.

"We lived in Karen, on what had once been Karen Blixen's farm," I said.

"And did you have a view of the Ngong Hills?"

Although surprised at her knowledge of this detail, I responded, "Absolutely. The five hills, linked together like the knuckles on a hand, a little south of the sunset. Kasmis, Oljoro, Onyote, Olotien and Lamwia. Hills sacred to the Maasai, marking the edge of the Rift Valley. That was the view from the veranda, across the stream that Blixen describes in *Out of Africa*, near where she and Finch Hatton shot the two lions that were troubling the families that lived on her farm. How come you are familiar with Karen Blixen and her farm?"

"Oh, I have often imagined I was there. I love Karen Blixen's writing and have read almost everything she wrote. *Out of Africa* is not my favourite, but I still loved the descriptions of her farm, of the hills, of flying with Finch Hatton. Actually, my favourites are her short stories, *Seven Gothic Tales*, especially *The Dreamers*. She was a wonderful writer, you know. When Hemingway received his Nobel Prize for Literature, he said that he would have been happier if the prize had gone to 'that beautiful writer Isak Dinesen' whom he called *la Sirena de Copenhagen.*"

"Why do you prefer her short stories?" I was not even aware she had written and published short stories.

"While I was studying for my Masters, I took a course with Alberto Paredes, a Mexican literature professor. We studied Quixote. One evening, at a dinner after graduation, I told Paredes that what I enjoyed most about Quixote was the many short stories within the greater story. He was the one who recommended Blixen to me, 'for her special talent at capturing a moment', he said. He was right. She could distil the essence of a moment, and from there create an elixir, a potion, a spell."

"Indeed, seated on the floor before the fireplace, casting the spell of the story-teller over Finch Hatton, like Scheherazade," I paused, intrigued. "And why the Ngong Hills?" I asked.

"They seem to me to symbolize an Africa that she would never be a part of. Even though she lived on the flanks of the hills. Even though she flew over the hills in the evening with Finch Hatton. Even though she buried him there, it was Maasailand, it would never be hers. As much as she loved Kenya, the Ngong Hills, the herd of buffaloes that lived on the hills, she would never be part of that world."

I was astonished. Here in Mexico City, a woman who had never been to Africa, who was entirely urban, had tapped into a vein that coursed somewhere deep within my soul – that sense of being part of something tinged with a sense of exclusion. My response was a non sequitur:

"There are still buffalo in the hills, you know, or at least there were when last I was there."

"How long ago was that?" she asked.

"Oh, maybe 20 years."

"Isn't it time to go back, to reconnect?"

That Christmas, 2010, I invited Angelica to Kenya with me. I was the guide. It was my job to see that she saw everything. But it was I who saw with new eyes, through her eyes, and the wonder of my youth returned. I took her to an area where I had often seen buffalo. Not the Ngong Hills – there are no buffalo there now – but to a plain near Nakuru. Sure enough, just as they were forty years ago, a herd of buffalo was grazing quietly, chomping on the grass, snorting through their large, wet nostrils. We were downwind. I left the Land Rover and advanced some thirty yards closer to take a photo. No signs of alarm, no twitching of the ears or raising of the nostrils. I beckoned her to join me, quietly, carefully, discreetly. When she was by my side, and we were crouched, peering through the long grass at these magnificent animals whose horns are thick as the thighs of an athlete, I turned to her and whispered: "If they charge, run to that tree and scamper up. They will fret a little and then leave you." Poor Angelica. I don't think she had ever been so frightened, but I was sure that they would not charge.

We watched flamingos at Lake Nakuru landing in the hundreds, blotting the sky pink. We saw hyena eating the carcass of a buffalo they had killed. We were enchanted by a pair of camels appearing mysteriously on a dune on the Lamu beach, silhouetted by the setting sun. And with each encounter, I came closer to my roots.

Had I been alone I would not have been so enchanted. Errol Trzebinski writes that Denys Finch Hatton was "a valuable enzyme" in Karen Blixen's development as a writer, that he "leavened"[e] her life, opening up new worlds. As is true in many love stories, this was also true for both Angelica and for me. She learned about wilderness, I learned "to read a book in the spirit in which it asks to be read." But it went further because I also found, through Angelica, a new appreciation of a world that I had loved and lost. Love means seeing things through the eyes of another, and sharing her emotions. Angelica taught me to reconnect, to find that world again.

---

e   Errol Trzebinski: *Silence will Speak. A Study of the Life of Denys Finch Hatton and His Relationship With Karen Blixen* (1977)

CHAPTER 2

THE SUN SETS ON KENYA'S HAPPY VALLEY

1920´s - 1952

In September 1946, a man born Kamau wa Ngengi, boarded the steamer, Alcantara, registering himself as "Jomo Kenyatta, Anthropologist", departing from England and bound for Mombasa. When Kenyatta landed in Mombasa in 1946, he stepped ashore, fell to his knees, scooped up the soil of his native land, and symbolically held it to his chest. There is no doubt that Kenyatta was well aware of the power of symbols, and that he had believed for some time that his destiny was to unite Kenya against the common enemy, the British rulers.

Six months later, John Harry Barclay Nihill and his wife Nuala boarded the steam vessel Modasa in Hull, England, also bound for Mombasa with stops in Malta, Suez, Port Said, and Aden. Built in 1920 by the British India Steam Navigation Company for passage to India with one funnel, two masts, and twin screws, the Modasa reached a maximum speed of 13.5 knots. Little did Barclay know that he was to be hurled into the cauldron of Kenya's struggle for independence. Kenyatta's path and that of John Harry Barclay Nihill were to intersect on several occasions over the next five years.

Unlike the jaded aristocrats who had populated Kenya since its earliest days as a British Colony, Barclay was of humble beginnings. Grandson of a Navy doctor, son of an Anglican Minister, he was left with a mother, four sisters and no father at the age of four. His life must have been oppressively restrictive, surrounded by spinster sisters and a matronly, deeply religious, and penuriously pensioned widow. But he had a quick mind and a diligent streak that won him a scholarship to Felsted, a well-respected private boarding school, and then to Cambridge where he not only ran the three mile event on his college track team but rose to the post of President of the Cambridge Students' Union, a significant achievement, especially considering his background.

During his last year at Cambridge, the Great War broke out, and upon graduating he was enlisted in the Royal Irish Fusiliers. While billeted in Dublin, he met and fell in love with one Nuala O'Carroll, a feisty, bright, young woman of Irish stock. A member of the first class of women to be admitted to Trinity College, Dublin, Nuala had studied Mathematics. It was a most improbable union. She was Catholic, from a privileged Irish family. Her father was the President of the Royal College of Surgeons in Dublin, President of the Zoological Society, and so on and so forth. Barclay had barely a shilling to his name, and, worse, he was from a devout Anglican family. Letters from his mother indicate a passionate belief that Catholics were close to the devil and that he should avoid mingling with them, let alone court a Catholic girl.

Before he embarked for the front, Barclay formally requested Nuala's hand in marriage from her father, Joseph O'Carroll. While he received signs of approval, his future father-in-law suggested that the two young lovers should carefully consider the complication involved in a marriage between a Catholic girl and an Anglican man. With this admonition from the father of his beloved, Barclay set off for the trenches of Ypres, where he was gassed, suffered from "trench foot" and won a Military Cross (second only to the Victoria Cross) for bravery. Upon his return, he renewed his courtship of Nuala, converted to Catholicism, married, and sought employment at the English Bar.

At Cambridge, Barclay had studied law, but, although he graduated with a First (High Honors), he was not welcomed with open arms by the English bar, which was, predictably, closed to those who did not come from the right families. Instead, he was shuttled off to the Colonial Service. His first post was as Attorney General of Hong Kong. He and Nuala lived on the Island of Macau, adjacent to Hong Kong. From Macau, he rode the ferry to the Hong Kong courthouse. My uncle, John Nihill, and my father, Alan Nihill, were born in Macau, and spent their youth moving periodically, to Iraq, British Guiana, west Africa and beyond.

The Kenya that greeted Barclay and Nuala upon their arrival in 1946 was like a long dormant volcano about to erupt. Standing on the rim of the volcano looking across miles of African plains, one had the sense of timeless balance between man and beast. But, beneath that surface, not yet apparent to the white colonial rulers, the unrest simmered, ready to burst forth with terrifying violence.

KENYA: THE HAPPY VALLEY

Since the turn of the century, the third sons and black sheep of England's aristocracy had been sent to Kenya to find their fortune or to be exiled, as insurance against them further shaming the family name. While the eldest son inherited the peerage, the baronetcy or the family estate, and the second son found a comfortable, well-endowed life within the Church of England, third sons had to marry well or find opportunity elsewhere. Kenya provided a perfect destination for these less fortunate but pedigreed gentlemen.

On the long steamer ride south to Cape Town and on to Kenya, a cabin with a window on the port which provided a view of the African coast as one travelled, was dubbed POSH, the acronym for Port Out, Starboard Home. Trunks packed with Royal Doulton china, family heirloom silverware, and portraits of heavily moustachioed ancestors standing beside their seated and demurely-clothed wives, made their precarious journey around the Cape of Good Hope and back up the eastern coast of Africa to the port of Mombasa.

The ocean voyage took several months. Long, languid days, gentlemen dressed in waistcoat, tails, high collared shirt and bow tie, the steamer plodding south through excruciatingly steamy equatorial waters. One might have the good fortune to encounter a young lady on her journey to join her betrothed, or better yet, returning to join her family after some years at a French "finishing school", enchanting in layers of white or cream-colored silk, absent-mindedly twirling her delicate parasol as she protected herself from the damaging rays of the sun. But even she was off limits, typically accompanied by that maiden aunt whose nose for troublesome young men had kept her chastity in place, and who was even more keenly attuned to the protection of her young protégé on the journey south. Imagine the ennui, the lassitude, the yearning for adventure or for the companionship of a kindred spirit of the tender sex, and you can imagine the pent up energy with which these testosterone-filled third sons reached the shores of Kenya.

Upon arrival in Mombasa, the eager colonists were greeted with a ten-gun salute from the old cannons of Fort Jesus, built by the

Portuguese in 1596, and still guarding the harbour entrance. Their numerous trunks were unloaded in the sweltering sun by Swahili workers in loincloths, and placed on the train from Mombasa to Nairobi. The train line had been built at the turn of the century, using Indian laborers and Indian 1000 millimeter gauge line. The train left Mombasa at afternoon tea time and arrived at Nairobi station the next morning. For the early settlers, the train ride was gruelling. There was no passageway connecting the compartments, and passengers were essentially secluded in their rooms between stops. A fine red dust crept into the rooms so that passengers arrived covered with a kind of red powder that matted the hair and gave one a slightly painted look. In those early days, the train would often stop to permit the gentlemen to stretch their legs and to bag a trophy rhino or even a lion. But by the 1930s the train had been spruced up, a passageway added, and smart new engines led the winding snake. During the day the compartments contained a comfortable bench seat and a small table by the window. But after the tea service, served on English china, the white-gloved railway butler pulled out a bunk bed, converted the bench into another bed, and lit the lights for the evening. Passengers sipped gin and tonics – *"You should try it my dear. Everyone here drinks the stuff. The quinine in the tonic keeps the mosquitoes away, you know."* – as the sun went down over the Tsavo plains, and then a five course dinner: soup, a fillet of fresh fish, followed by roast lamb with mint sauce, fruit salad, and a dessert, all served on cut crystal and silverware. As dawn broke, the train was chunting through the plains to the east of Nairobi, teeming with game. Even today giraffe, zebra, wildebeest and a range of antelope are visible from the comfort of your compartment.

Arriving at Nairobi, the serenity was shattered. Descending from the train one was surrounded by jostling, shouting crowds pushing carts, carrying bags, offering rides to the New Stanley Hotel. If one was fortunate, or connected, it is likely that he was met by friends on horseback, possibly with a wagon in tow. The mountain of suitcases and boxes were unloaded and placed on ox carts for the precarious long journey "up country" to the White Highlands.

Not all the colonists who set foot in Kenya were landed gentry, even in the early days. There was a good sprinkling of reprobates of high or moderate birth who had sullied, or had a tendency to sully, the family name. Unlike their socially inferior counterparts who were sent to Australia on convict ships, these black sheep were quietly enrolled in obscure government positions in places like Nanyuki or Eldoret where no amount of trouble was likely to embarrass the remaining family members who populated the salons of London. The mixture of these two groups – titled gentry with too much money, and those with a tendency to disreputable adventure – was to form the basis for the Kenyan reputation for libertine and outrageous behaviour.

The "White Highlands" of Kenya, running in a V from Nairobi up to Mount Kenya to the west and the Rift Valley to the East, was their playground. Naivasha, Gilgil, Nakuru, and Njoro, names redolent of an historic past. The Aberdare Mountains, Laikipia and Thompson's Falls. Tea and coffee plantations abounded. Wild game roamed free across the land, and a gentleman's day was more likely spent hunting lion or buffalo, or galloping after jackals behind fox-hounds imported from England by Jim Elkington in 1913, than attending to the farm. This was best left in the hands of a foreman. Many of these foremen were Boers or "*rooineks*" who had trekked up from South Africa by oxcart, a journey of many months and extraordinary hardship, similar in scope and challenge to the treks of the early American pioneers who journeyed west in the footsteps of Lewis and Clark. Others were simple, middle class Englishmen, often down on their luck financially, who moved to Kenya for another chance. Men like Jos Grant, father of the early Kenya writer, Elspeth Huxley, and, in the aftermath of the Great War, a large number of ex-servicemen lured by the Kenya Government's offer of a 999 year lease of land in the White Highlands at a rent of ten cents an acre per year.

The Muthaiga Club was the weekend watering hole. Nestled below tall acacia trees by the Athi River on the north side of Nairobi – the side on which the highland plantations were all located – it was the rendezvous for the numerous characters who illuminated the Kenya social scene. Denys Finch Hatton and Lady Delamere (both minor aristocrats) often dined there, as did "Cape to Cairo Grogan", a troublemaker who was expelled from both his school and his college at Cambridge, but later redeemed himself, and earned the hand of his beloved in marriage, by walking from Cape Town to Cairo. Karen Dinesen and her husband Baron Bror Blixen – another miscreant of the first order – often drove over to Muthaiga even though their coffee farm was on the other side of town, the side where I was born and where the Ngong Hills overlooked Maasailand. Lord Errol, who was shot in 1941 by his lover's husband after he returned his companion (Errol's wife) to her home adjacent to the Blixens' farm, passed his last evening dancing at the Muthaiga Club.

If you believe that writers are the mirrors of a society, the history of Kenyan writers of this era provides an interesting reflection.

The writers were few, and those whose works are still read are all women. Elspeth Huxley describes the earliest days of the white settlers in *The Flame Trees of Thika,* a delightful account of a young girl (aged 5 to about 15) growing up wild on the farm near Thika where the family settled in 1912.

Beryl Markham, whose family moved to Kenya in 1906, writes about her life as an aviator, carrying the mails and medical supplies to hurriedly cleared airstrips in the bush, a kind of Saint Exupéry of the East African savannah. This career culminates with her historic solo transatlantic flight from England to the New World, ending in a crash on the shores of Nova Scotia, described beautifully in *West with the Night.*

And, of course, there is Karen Blixen.

All of them were frighteningly independent women, who loved fiercely both Kenya and their men. But where are the men writers? Why do we not have any men putting pen to paper in these formative years of the colony? Some of my friends argue that the men were all working too hard, and that only the women had the time for the luxury of writing. But that argument does not hold up when you read the accounts of the lives led by the women, who were as active as the men. Others might argue that after the first phase of pioneering settlers, and those that came in the years after the Great War, the men who decided to migrate to Kenya self se-lected, and were by and large more interested in the hunting, the outdoors, and the easy life than they were either in hard physi-cal labor or the introspection of writing. Be that as it may, these three women, and others who came after them like Joy Adamson (*Born Free)* and Marjorie Macgoye (*Coming to Birth*), were strong, passionate women, who set a tone for the Kenyan girl that was still prevalent among the youth of my generation.

Karen Blixen cast a long shadow. Her love affair with Denys Finch Hatton is part of the cultural mythology of the European Kenyan. He, dashing, unencumbered, at one with the land and the peoples of Kenya. She, beautiful (before she was ravaged by the syphilis that she contracted from her philandering, drunken husband), poetic and a storyteller. In *Out of Africa* she writes lovingly of the evenings spent weaving tales and casting spells that temporarily captivated the nomadic Finch Hatton sitting mesmerized at her feet.

The British settlers, and other white residents of Kenya, felt no sense of Kenyan identity. They toasted the Queen on her birthday, they celebrated St. George's day, and lit fireworks on November 5 in remembrance of the night a group of English Catholics led by Guy Fawkes attempted, unsuccessfully, to blow up the Houses of Parliament. Kenya was not a country to which they owed an allegiance. It was merely the place where they, fervent British subjects, happened to live. If, as the French anthropologist, Emmanuel Todd has suggested, identity is a function of five elements: language, customs, ethnicity, geography and religion, the white settlers shared none of these elements with the African population, except geography. Even geographically the settlers segregated themselves from other Kenyans, living in exclusive whites only areas. Nor did the African residents of Kenya feel a Kenyan identity. For the most part, they identified themselves as Kikuyu or Kalenjin, Luo or Maasai. Their identity and allegiance was tribal, and, in a way, the white residents of Kenya were merely another tribe within the geographic boundaries of Kenya, a tribe that, like the Maasai, crossed country boundaries and felt no national allegiance.

A 1950 Snapshot

Three years after Barclay and Nuala settled in to Nairobi, my father, Alan, brought his new bride Jeannine, to join them and build
a home in the Colony. Kenya was still the Jewel in the Crown of
the British Colonies, and, with the prominent position that Barclay
held, it made sense for them to strengthen the family roots there. I
was born in 1950, and my sister Caitlín in 1952. We lived in a little
ranger's cottage in Karen, part of what had been Karen Blixen's
farm, on the fringe of what is now Nairobi National Park. Our
neighbors to the north and west were Kikuyu, whose women were
forever working, carrying loads of wood in sacks on their backs
supported by leather bands that cut deep impressions into their
foreheads. To the south and east were the Maasai, their young *mo-
ran* tall, beautiful, athletic, a blanket across their shoulders, a loin
cloth around their waists, a spear, a beaded headband, and shoes
cut from the hide of a cow or a wildebeest, without a shred of fear
in their hearts; their women decorated with heavy circles of bead
necklaces, earrings that hung from their extended earlobes, carrying their ration of water in gourds draped across their chests.

In the white, British Colonial sanctuary of Karen, Kenya was
all horses and gymkhanas, polo ponies and Pimms. The thatched,
single story homes extended over acres of barely tamed wilderness,
lush with frangipanis, orchids, gladioli and hibiscus, the large acacia
trees providing shade against the equatorial sun. Brilliant purple
and rainbow-striped starlings nodded their heads as they pecked
seeds greedily from the bird feeders. Sacred ibis, black heads and
long curved black beaks contrasting with their fluffy white bodies, flew majestically across the broad, manicured lawns. From the
back yard terrace, the Ngong Hills rose splendidly, teeming with

buffalo and giraffe, and in their foothills lay the northern tip of Maasailand, the heart of Kenya where man and wild animal lived in timeless harmony.

Almost all the homes had stables attached, some with a string of polo ponies, others with race horses, and others with jumpers and show horses. In the early mornings the *syces*, or grooms, exercised the horses, walking them down the wooded lanes of Karen, and then galloping them on the open flays that lay beside the Langata forest. In the late afternoons, groups gathered for tennis on the private courts that graced the large gardens, or for an evening workout in the paddock, followed by cocktails, and possibly a round or two of bridge. Weekends, Alan and Jeannine attended the races or the show jumping and dressage events, she dressed in a silk dress and embroidered hat, he in riding britches and scarf.

My birth certificate reads Martin Dumonteil Nihill. The Dumonteil a nod to my mother's French origin, and the Martin, an accommodation, a name that could be handled equally in French and English. But this did not satisfy grandmother Helène. *"Pourquoi Martin?"* she asked, *"Martin c'est un ours, a teddy bear, no? Et un peu bête aussi."* She was not happy with the name, which was a common name for a clumsy bear in French folklore. Alan's response, a little supercilious, was: "Well, how about Julian? That has a sense of poetry, like a slim volume of verse." I don't think Jeannine had a say, and, in any event, Julian worked well in French. When Caitlín was born, Alan was into his Irish origins, and wanted his daughter named after Caitlín Ní Huallacháin, the protagonist of Yeats' play of the same name, in which Caitlín is a representation of Mother Ireland, a symbol of Irish nationalism, in her struggle for freedom from British rule.

Early photographs taken in Karen show us alternating between ridiculous outfits – I, in a sailor's suit, Caitlín in muslin and a bonnet – and running naked through the garden chasing chameleons and caterpillars.

What our family, the colonial rulers and the new immigrant white settlers did not see, was the volcano that was about to explode.

CHAPTER 3

THE CHIEF JUSTICE, THE PRESIDENT,

AND THE MAU MAU

THE RISE OF THE MAU MAU

Immediately after the end of World War II there was a spike in English settler immigration and the cost of products grown on settlers' farms rose rapidly. Farming became more lucrative and large areas, especially along the Rift Valley and on the slopes of Mount Kenya, were opened up for white settler farming. The need for more farmers was met in large part by former British army officers looking for a way out of the damp, depressed State that was England in 1945. Before this expansion, the farms were worked by large numbers of Kikuyu "squatters", or tenant farmers, on white settler lands. But with this newfound prosperity, the settlers, especially those in the rich Rift Valley farms, sought to expand the area they farmed, and large numbers of Kikuyu peasants were evicted and left homeless. Some of these returned to the Kikuyu homelands (areas reserved for Kikuyu, particularly around Mount Kenya and the Aberdare Mountains), where their presence increased the burden of an unsustainable land shortage among the Kikuyu farming population. In 1948, 25,000 white settlers owned over 12,000 square miles of the White Highlands, the plateau north of Nairobi, to the west of the Mount Kenya, where the soil was wonderfully fertile, the climate temperate, and the white settler population entrenched. The 1,250,000 Kikuyu, the original inhabitants of the region, owned a mere 2,000 square miles of this paradise.

By mid-1947, shortly after he landed in Mombasa, Kenyatta was elected President of the newly formed Kenya African Union (KAU), which was to become the formal Kikuyu mouthpiece for African independence. But, as is so often the case, the forces of independence were various and at odds with one another.

Kenyatta and the KAU represented the educated, and essentially conservative, wing of the independence movement. To the right of the KAU were the chiefs, many of them Christian, and most in thrall to the colonial government. Among these was Chief Warahui wa Kungu, Paramount Chief of the Central Province, the owner of substantial property in Kiambu, immediately west of Nairobi, and the colonial government's main point person within the African community. To the left of the KAU were the men who were to form the Mau Mau, comprised of two elements: displaced agricultural workers, and residents of the East Nairobi slums.

In 1948, the Forty Group, a collection of ex-military African Kenyans committed to the overthrow of colonial rule, was formed, and established itself as a kind of Robin Hood gang operating in Eastlands, the slums to the east of the city. Between 1948 and 1952, some 28,000 Kikuyu males migrated into the Eastlands area. This was fertile ground for radicals, and its leaders quickly took advantage. In the mid 1940's, the residents of Olenguruone, an area northwest of Nairobi, home to many displaced Kikuyu, revitalized the traditional Kikuyu practice of "oathing", a practice that many whites saw as akin to a secret society pledge. Starting in 1950, the leaders in the Eastlands slums, adopted the practice and rapidly proceeded to "oath" large groups of Eastlands residents, and then expanded the practice north into the Kikuyu heartland. By the mid '50s, ninety percent of the Kikuyu, Meru and Embu people had been oathed.

Starting about 1950 the Mau Mau began to make their presence felt among the Kikuyu population. They used force to obtain food, arms and safe houses, and set fire to the homes of Kikuyus in Nairobi who refused to take an oath of allegiance to the Mau Mau rebellion. Between May and September of 1952, there was a rash of murders of Africans loyal to, or aligned with the government. The new Governor, Evelyn Baring, arrived in Kenya in September 1952, and was briefed that during the past three months twenty-four headmen and thirty-six potential witnesses in Mau Mau cases, all Africans, had been murdered. Law and order were collapsing. Then, in October 1952, the Mau Mau emerged with terrifying force to terrorize the white population. On October 3, 1952, the first white victim of Mau Mau attacks was hacked to death in her house in Thika. Days later, on October 7, Paramount Chief Waruhiu, who sided with the government, was dragged from his car and shot in broad daylight in the streets of Nairobi. On October 27, Eric Bowyer, an old settler, was found murdered and disemboweled in his home. On November 22, Commander Meiklejohn and his wife were shot in their home near Nakuru.

The Whites were terrified and belligerent. Governor Baring declared a State of Emergency on October 20, and rounded up some 180 supposed Mau Mau leaders. The British had identified Kenyatta as the ringleader, the man they had to convict and send far from the political limelight. He was whisked off, in a military plane, to a remote outpost of Northern Kenya, and then, on

November 18, he was formally charged with the offence of "managing an illegal society", the Mau Mau. The trial was set for the 24th, just 6 days later. It is far from clear whether, or to what extent Kenyatta's KAU party was related to, or was even supportive of, the Mau Mau movement. But in the eyes of Kenya's frightened colonial settlers they were largely synonymous. Kenyatta, and the KAU, stood between the two factions emerging in the Kenyan independence movement – the conservative Christian leaders and the militant, restless radicals who were to form the Mau Mau.

On many occasions Kenyatta spoke out against the activities of the Mau Mau. It is probable that he was not involved in any of their more violent activity, but his voice of reason was drowned out by the stories of Mau Mau activity. The gruesomeness of the murders; the stories of the oathing ceremonies which involved animal sacrifice, oaths to kill anyone opposed to Mau Mau, including other Africans; oaths to rid the country of the white man; and tales of torture, the gouging of eyes, the bathing in blood, many of them true, elicited in the white population the deepest, darkest fears of the unknown, of savagery, and witchcraft.

Kenyatta's trial took place in December 1952 and January 1953. The Kenya Government did all it could to shackle the defense. The case was tried in one of the remotest parts of the Colony, Kipenguria. The defending attorneys' access to their clients was severely limited. Witnesses were presented without warning, requiring the defense to scramble to find opposing testimony. Worst of all, the lead prosecution witness, Rawson Macharia was suborned. His testimony, it was discovered some years later, was purchased by the Government and paid for in air fare to England for him and his family, two years at an English University, housing for him and his family, and a government post upon his return. These facts, and the contractual agreement between the Government and Macharia, were not discovered until 1958, by which time, of course, the verdict had been reached, and Kenyatta was safely out of the way. Ten defense witnesses contradicted Macharia's testimony, but Judge Thacker stated in his summing up that he had "no hesitation" to "disbelieve ten witnesses for the Defense and believe one for the Prosecution." Macharia testified in December 1952. By New Year's Day he was already in England.

On Monday, January 26, 1953 Kenyatta entered the witness box. But Fate played her hand to stack the cards against him. Two days earlier, on the evening of Saturday, January 24, the following scene played out. The facts in this account have all been carefully researched from contemporary newspaper articles, the transcript of the trial of the attackers, and several books on the Mau Mau. In addition, I was able to interview a few people with first hand knowledge of the facts including members of the family who took over the Ruck farm. The dialogue, however, is my own, based on my knowledge of Kenya settler families and on what I imagine would have been the conversation that evening.

THE RUCK FAMILY MASSACRE

Roger and Esme Ruck sat on the porch of their compact, shingle-roofed, two story house on the fringes of the forest above Lake Naivasha. They had named their home Quantoca Combe, a combe being an old English word for a deep, lush valley. The house faced west, overlooking the lake and the valley below. Behind them, and above them, rose the Aberdare Mountains, home to Mount

Kinangkop and the foothills of Mount Kenya. Over 10,000 feet high, the plateau known as the Kinangkop, was the heart of the White Highlands, whose rich soil and temperate climate earned it the reputation of being a colonial paradise. This was cloud forest. Giant aromatic cedar trees with their gnarled trunks cloaked in moss towered above the thick green bushes and undergrowth. In the mornings a hoar frost settled on the lawn and low mist hung below the trees, burning off as the sun rose. From the porch they looked upon a carefully manicured lawn, lined with flowerbeds brimming with geraniums, agapanthus and gladioli. Orange butterflies, trimmed with black, sucked at the stamens of the hibiscus, and fire finches fluttered in to sip from the teak water bowl that Mbogo, one of the farm hands, had carved for Esme. Below the lawn lies a gorge, also thick with cedar trees festooned with grey beards of lichen, like dark green spears stabbing the evening sky, and through the gorge runs a tributary of the Minja River. By the stream there are wild olives, a lighter, brownish color. Now, at the end of the day, the sun was setting over the lake. A cool breeze crept up the slope, carrying with it the sounds of wild life preparing for the night. Colobus monkeys leapt from tree to tree rustling the branches, and occasionally the Rucks caught sight of their graceful, long, white and black tails as they flew from one branch to another. Turacos swooped gracefully in huge arcs from the tops of the pogo and cedar trees, alighting on the lawn that Roger had cut from the forest. The turacos enchanted Esme. Seated on the high trees, their green and blue bodies glistened in the speckled sunlight. But when they flew down to the lawn, the undersides of their wide, open wings burned red, blood red, lighting up the sky. As the orange sky turned to dark crimson, the cicadas began their deafening hum, the sound of a thousand wings vibrating together in unison. Piercing the cicada melody were the blood curdling shrieks of the male tree hyrax, that would rise to a crescendo an hour or so after dark.

Mbogo had brought the cattle in for the night, to corral them into the *manyatta* where the long, sharp needles of the thorn tree brush would protect them from lions, leopards and other predators.

Roger took a gulp of his Tusker beer and then, turning to Esme, commented:

"Went over to the sawmill today to have some of our trunks cut for the new stables. Bumped into Tony Pape. He is now running the local volunteer Police Force, you know."

"Of course, darling. And how is Tony doing?"

"Well, he told me that last night they were on a recce, him and a couple of the lads, and they surprised a group of *watu* meeting in the woods not 3 miles from our house. Illegal, of course. About 40 of them. Tony and the KPR[f] guys were able to capture twenty-two of them, but the rest got away. A couple of them had guns, and Tony was shot at but was not harmed."

"That's awful, dear. Were they Mau Mau?"

"Can't tell for sure, but you know that these meetings are illegal, and that if these guys are caught with even one round of ammo, much less a pistol, it's the hangman's noose. My guess, and Tony agrees, they're probably the same bunch that killed old Bowyer back in October."

"My God, that's terrible. I hate to think that this dreadful Mau Mau business is closing in on us."

---

f   Kenya Police Reserve. Some 4,800 part time individuals, and an additional 2,000 officers, primarily from the settler class, who formed a quasi-volunteer force that policed the White Highlands, and acted independently against the Mau Mau.

"Well, seems like it's getting awfully close. Tony tells me that what they do is infiltrate a farm or a village and then make all the Kikuyu workers take an oath to drive out the white man."

Roger's brown and white spaniel, Flynn, bounded up to him, nuzzling his nose against Roger's thigh. Roger gave Flynn a friendly pat and then muttered, more to himself than to Esme, "Dreadful thing this blasted Oathing stuff."

"What did you say, Darling? Couldn't hear you for the shrieking of the tree hyrax out there."

"Oathing. Damned bad stuff. Drinking blood. Vowing to force the whites out of Kenya. Pitting black against white and Kikuyu against Kikuyu. A couple of days ago, Jock was telling me.... I saw him in Karimjee's store.... Jock was telling me that there were reports of Oathing ceremonies near Mount Kinangkop. The Special Services guys told him that that fellow, Kimathi, had been seen in the vicinity. Bloody shame really. Who the hell do they think made this land the way it is. Not them. That's for certain. Its our bloody sweat and toil that planted coffee, built clinics, made their children safe at night."

"Now, Roger, dear, you don't think that was what was going on at the meeting that the KDP broke up last night, do you, some kind of Mau Mau oathing stuff?"

"Who knows, but I will say that they will have a hard time with our *watu*. We treat them well, most of them have been with us a couple of years, and I believe that they are all loyal."

Roger took another gulp of his Tusker beer. "Good man, that Nderito." Roger commented, referring to the *syce* who cared for their horses. "Not like those damned Mau Mau. You know, yesterday morning, when Michael fell from Redanda down by where the path to Kongoni crosses the stream, Nderito carried him all the way up to the house."

"I feel the same about the house staff, too," said Esme. "Chira brought her mother into the clinic this afternoon. The old lady has lost most of her teeth and her gums are infected. Common problem. They think that chewing that dreadful *miraa* plant will help, but it doesn't. We will never change the way these people live, Roger. The best we can do is ease their pain."

Esme was a doctor, but at this time of night her preferred medicine was a J&B Whisky on the rocks, which she sipped between sentences. Esme ran a small clinic on the farm where she administered medicines to the local African, mainly Kikuyu, population, and daily she received the hugs of thanks of a grateful people. She was trim, blond, vivacious and quite the center of attention when she and Roger would occasionally journey into Naivasha for a drink at the Gymkhana Club. Roger was a farmer. He was 38, and had lived in Kenya since he was a child. He had built his farm with love and meticulous care. Each year, if the crops did not fail and he had some money left over, he cleared a new area for planting, laid another row of bricks to expand the walls of his home, built a new stable for his horses or hut for his workers. The farm had grown over the years, stone upon stone, cleared area upon cleared area. But now life was becoming more difficult with the increasing reports of attacks by the Mau Mau.

"You know, only the other day Chira was telling me how much she enjoyed the tomatoes that they were growing in their *shamba*."

"You're right, Es, I know, but still makes me bloody nervous. I know our *watu* are decent and loyal, but you can't be too careful."

Roger polished off the rest of his Tusker, placing the bottle on the small table by his chair with a thud. A sense of finality.

"Let's go in and get to bed. I have a long day tomorrow. Have to take Pygmalion in to the vet. She lost a shoe last week and seems to have developed an infection in her hocks."

As they went back into the house, Esme turned to Chira, their cook:

"*Asante*, Chira. Time for you to get some sleep. Be sure that the outside gates are locked before you go to bed."

"*Ndiyo, Memsahib. Lala na salaama*" Sleep well.

Esme went ahead to Michael's room. Although only six years old, Michael loved to ride, and especially loved his pony, Redanda. Most mornings Esme would start the day with Michael, visiting the stables where Nderito, the *syce*, was cleaning out the stalls. Michael enjoyed joining in the ritual of brushing Redanda's mane, standing on an upturned box to reach the pony's neck. Sometimes Roger, Esme and Michael would ride out across the streams and woods of the Kinangkop, carrying lunch and picnicking by a trout stream where Roger would cast for trout in the hope of adding to their lunch. But, more often, Michael rode Redanda while Nderito led the other horses by their reins as he walked them down the forest paths for exercise.

Esme tiptoed into Michael's room, turned out the gas on his lantern, and kissed him on the forehead. His teddy bear lay beside him. Esme moved it up to the head of the bed where it could watch over and protect her little boy.

Roger lingered, methodically checking the locks on all the doors. There had been a rash of attacks recently, mostly on Kikuyus who worked with settlers, but on New Year's Eve, two old white settlers, Charles Fergusson and Dick Bingley, had been murdered as they sat down to New Year's Eve dinner together. The next day, two elderly widows, Kitty Hesselberger and Raynes Simpson, living alone near Nyeri were attacked in their living room. These two old gals fared better than their male counterparts. They had arranged their furniture so that they faced the entrance to the room, and had loaded shotguns by their sides. As the first member of the Mau Mau gang entered, Mrs. Simpson let fly, killing him as he stepped across the doorsill. Kitty Hesselberger, who was in the adjacent bathroom, heard the gunshots, fired through the wall, killing two more attackers. At this the point the gang made their escape, leaving their three dead comrades behind.

Roger extinguished the hurricane lamp in the living room, and, as he passed into the hallway leading to the kitchen and bedrooms, he picked up his shotgun, checked to see that it was loaded, and carried it back with him toward the bedroom. At that moment he heard a tentative "*Hodi, Bwana*" and a knock on the front door. It was Nderito's voice. What could be the problem? He turned and stepped back into the living room. "*Unataka nini*? What do you want?" he asked.

"They have caught a man they say is with Mau Mau, Bwana, and say you must take him to police station."

Leaving the shotgun propped against the bedroom door, but carrying his biretta pistol with him, Roger unlocked the front door and stepped outside. Beyond the immediate light of his lantern hung a curtain of darkness. The night was unusually quiet. The birds had stopped their singing. No goats were bleating or dogs barking. Even the cicadas had turned in for the night. Roger wondered why there was not the usual chatter of voices, especially given that a man had been captured.

Without warning, a howl, as of a hundred hyenas, tore the night. Out of the shadow beyond his lantern's glow burst a horde of maniacal men, waving *pangas* and clubs. In an instant they fell on Roger. One man hacked at his legs. He fell to the ground, his screams both furious and terrified. Blows rained down on his head. As he fell, the frenzied attackers hacked at his arms, legs and face. In a minute his head was lying yards from his body, his eyes were gouged out, blood pulsing from the sockets in spurts.

Hearing the screams, Esme rushed out of her room, saw the shotgun, grabbed it, and ran to the aid of her fallen husband. She barely snapped the barrel closed before she, too, was attacked by the bloody gang. Their howling increased, frenetically, almost demoniacally, as they hacked at her and chopped her down in her stride.

Leaving Roger and Esme in pools of their blood, members of the gang burst into the house. They grabbed the guns and ammunition but not anything else. They were not there to steal. They knew where they were headed, to the room of the sleeping boy. Dragging him out of bed, they killed him quickly with swift strokes of their *pangas*, leaving him mutilated on the ground outside the house.

And then they left. Quiet returned to the Kinangkop. Except for the shrieking of a lone tree hyrax.

As a pebble thrown in a pond causes ripples that reach far beyond the splash point; as an earthquake on one side of the Indian Ocean causes gigantic waves to crash onto the shore of the East African coast; so this massacre impacted my life, and those of many who were living in Kenya at the time, in ways that none of us could have foreseen.

Kenyatta is Convicted. We move to Tanganyika
News of the murders spread faster than drums or wildfire. Monday morning the East African Standard carried photographs of Michael

Ruck's bloodstained teddy bear sitting at the head of young Michael's bed, and the gruesome details of the killings. The white settlers were incensed, and literally up in arms. Several hundred of them drove down to Nairobi Sunday evening and on Monday morning they marched to Government House, brandishing weapons and demanding more aggressive action by the authorities. That afternoon, some 200 settlers met with their representative on the Legislative Council, Michael Blundell, and voted almost unanimously (with three nay votes) in favor of the resolution that:

"there will be no peace in Kenya until control from the Colonial Office is severed, and that the Meeting demands government of Kenya by Kenyans, under European leadership."[g]

The profile of the settlers had changed markedly since the end of World War II. Some 20,000 Europeans moved to Kenya after the War. Many of them were mid level army officers who wished for a more exciting and prosperous life than that offered to them in England. They saw themselves as the "backbone of the Empire". General Erskine[1], the aristocratic military man sent to Kenya in 1953 to break the Mau Mau rebellion, and who found them to be a tiresome thorn in his side, referred to these newcomers, in correspondence to his wife, as "middle class sluts".[h] The Kenya writer, Ngugi wa Thiong'o called them "parasites in paradise".[i] Each description carried its grain of truth.

Kenyatta's trial ended March 10. In the subsequent days the mood in Kenya grew even darker. On March 26, a Mau Mau

---

g   The East African Standard, Tuesday January 14, 1953.

h   Carole Elkins, *Imperial Reckoning: The Untold Story of Britain's Gulag in Kenya p. 52.* Erskine also described Kenya to his wife as "a sunny land for shady people." Letter dated June 3, 1953, quoted in Anthony Clayton, *Counter-insurgency in Kenya 1952-1960* (NIROBI, 1976) P. 11

i   The Village Priest.

band attacked the Naivasha police station in the Rift Valley, making away with a large stash of weapons and ammunition. The same evening, some 3,000 Mau Mau men swept through Lari, a village whose chief was loyal to the Government. They burnt huts, hacked at man and beast with their *pangas*, and left 97 men, women and children dead. Even if Kenyatta had not been guilty, the political pressure to put him and others behind bars was overwhelming. On April 8, 1953, Judge Thacker found Jomo Kenyatta guilty, and he was sentenced to seven years hard labor. Like Macharia several months earlier, Judge Thacker, was promptly whisked out of the country after the trial, and received a "hardship bonus" of 20,000 Pounds Sterling for his efforts.

Kenyatta's attorneys filed an appeal, mostly on procedural grounds. It went first to an appeals court, known as the Supreme Court of Kenya, and then to the East African Court of Appeal, of which my grandfather, Barclay Nihill, was the President. The appeal was dismissed. Kenyatta and five co-defendants were sentenced to spend the next six and a half years in the remote desert village of Lokitaung, near Lake Turkana.

The colonial government had imprisoned the leader of the independence movement, but they had got the wrong man. In the forests around Mount Kenya and in the Aberdare Mountains, two men, more dangerous, more volatile, more violent than Kenyatta would ever be, were forming their bands of warriors: Dedan Kimathi, and Warahiu Itote, a.k.a. General China, the true, charismatic leaders of the Mau Mau.

Between 1950 and 1953, my father, Alan was the Manager of the East African Standard, Kenya's major newspaper, and, inevitably, viewed as a mouthpiece for colonial white propaganda. 1953 had been an extraordinarily difficult and divisive year in Kenya. In addition to the trial of Kenyatta, there had been the deaths of Fergusson, Bigley, the Ruck family and four other settler families. Thirty-seven men had been sentenced to death by hanging for their part in attacks on settlers and on a group of loyalist Christian Africans the night of Christmas Eve 1952. There had been the Lari massacre, and the conviction and hanging of 35 men accused of participating in that massacre, most of whom were tried in mass trials with minimal defense counsel. Tens of thousands of Kikuyu had been detained without trial and sent to detention camps in remote parts of Kenya for "rehabilitation." In the words of David Anderson, author of *Histories of the Hanged*, the definitive biography of the Mau Mau rebellion, Kenya had become "a police state." Against the backdrop of fear caused by the Declaration of the Emergency, these trials, and Alan's perceived position as an unofficial mouthpiece of the Government, Kenya was not an ideal place to raise a three year-old son, and his newborn sister. Early in 1954 the family moved to Dar-es-Salaam, Tanganyika where Alan accepted the post of Managing Director of the Tanganyika Standard, that country's main newspaper.

Some years ago I asked my mother why the family left Kenya.

"You know how nightmares sometimes start as the most beautiful dreams" she responded, "and then inexplicable things happen and the picture changes. That was Kenya in 1953. You were two, turning three. Beginning to talk and walk and to be a little person. Your good friend was Charles Erskine, the son of General "Bobbi" Erskine[j]. Your *ayah* was a lovely Kikuyu lady, Alice, who loved you and took great care of you. You were always exploring the garden, tasting the fruit, clapping at the butterflies."

---

j Jeannine was mistaken here. Charles Erskine was son of Derek Erskine, a relative.

"Butterflies, Mum? At two? I could hardly walk, I'm sure."

"Well, maybe not butterflies, but certainly caterpillars, then. You were always curious about caterpillars and butterflies. Caitlín was born in May 1952 and took much of my attention. Like you, she was a cheerful peaceful baby. Our little cabin on the edge of the park was small but cozy, and we felt completely peaceful listening to the roar of the lions and the howling of hyenas in the evenings. Then everything changed. Your father was an excellent horseman, and although we could not afford horses the good trainers and breeders wanted him to ride their horses and to compete in the shows. He won the Kenya Open Show Jumping championship two years in a row riding a horse owned by Jane Dunn, one of our neighbors. But, during 1953 he started staying later and later at the stables, and then the rumors started, and finally even I knew that he and Jane were having an affair."

"And that's why you left Kenya?" I asked incredulously, imagining that the situation could have been handled in different ways.

"Oh no, that's not why we left, but it was the beginning of the nightmare. The picture really started to go bad with the Ruck family murder. Alan's job was to report the news. But Erskine and others put a lot of pressure on him to tell the story from the government's point of view. You know, neither your grandfather nor your father felt comfortable with the way the government dealt with Kenyatta. There were many evenings when the two of them would sit late at the dinner table talking about Operation Jock Scott, the mass trials of the Lari defendants, the identity pass laws, and how the state of emergency was unconstitutional and counterproductive. But when the Ruck murder occurred the day before

Kenyatta was to take the stand in that trumped up trial, they were put in a very difficult position. After that Barclay and Nuala had twenty-four hour police guards. Barclay received threats to his life, and we felt under siege. The terrifying thing about the Mau Mau was that they would threaten the people who worked for you, your loyal servants, people who were part of your family, and would use them to enter your home. Especially if they were Kikuyu. I was so afraid that that would happen to us that I let Alice go and hired a Luo girl from near the Uganda border. One day, In November of 1953, the *askari* who was opening the gate to let me in told me that a man, "a Kikuyu", he said, had come around earlier asking whether we were home and where is the young *bwana?*" Who was this man? Why did he want to know your whereabouts? Was he part of the Mau Mau, come to take you or worse? I was hysterical and told your father that unless we left as a family, I would leave with the two of you. I had no idea where I would go, but I just knew Kenya was not safe for us.

That's why we left Kenya."

———

Many years later, my grandfather told me how impressed he was with Kenyatta's bearing, and although he was convinced that Kenyatta was indeed guilty, he cautioned me that the Judge's role is to apply the law, not to question its fairness or good sense. He was one white Kenyan who thought that the time had come to accelerate the path to Independence. He was in a minority at the time. Years later, during the Independence celebrations in 1963, they met again. Kenyatta expressed no resentment. He was gracious and welcoming. While his later years were tarnished by the influence of his greedy and corrupt third wife, Mama Ngina, Kenyatta remains in the pantheon of African leaders who sacrificed everything for the freedom of their people.

When one researches the story of one's ancestors, it is natural to hope to find nuggets that show them as heroic or generous, wise or powerful. Personally, I merely hoped for evidence that the good and generous man that I knew had exhibited his integrity, the integrity and commitment to truth and justice that I saw in him, in a public way. I did not find that evidence in this Court of Appeals judgment. Maybe the procedural point was too fine, the argument too weak, to carry the burden of overturning a six month trial. Maybe the political pressures were simply too great to ignore. Maybe Barclay, and the other justices, felt that Kenyatta had indeed lead the Mau Mau movement, even if only from afar, from a safe distance where he and his movement for African emancipation could benefit from the horrors of the Mau Mau without taking responsibility.

Spending the better part of the Christmas and Easter holidays with my grandparents between the ages of 10 and 16, I became very close to my grandfather. He was a good man. His commitment to justice, to the rights of the oppressed, to an open social structure in which the sons and daughters of miners and ministers could interact with, debate with, and be judged on equal terms with those of lords and squires, was apparent even to an inexperienced young teenager. I have the greatest respect for my grandfather and have named my son after him. But I sometimes wonder whether it is enough to be a Good man, especially if one could have been a Great man, a man who could have changed the course of history, or at least who could have so influenced it that other men's consciences would have been aroused to act differently. As Barclay told me on the last day I was with him, before I left for America, "while one can judge a man's actions, one cannot judge the man." Only God and that man's conscience know all the forces that played upon him as he acted. And only God and the man himself are fit to judge the man.[2]

CHAPTER 4

CHILDHOOD IN THE HAVEN OF PEACE

1953 – 1962

My parents met in 1948 at a Debutantes' Ball in Calcutta, India. Alan was an aide to the Governor of Bengal. Jeannine, at 19, was rather beautiful, and sent to find a husband.

JEANNINE

Jeannine was the oldest of three children born to Richard Morgan-Davies and Helène Dumonteil Lagrèze. Richard's father was of Welsh coal miner stock. Against all odds, he gained a scholarship to Cambridge, ran high hurdles for the University in the annual rivalry with Oxford, and graduated in 1914.

However, just as Kenya in 1930 was a playground for the dissolute offspring of English aristocrats; just as black people in Alabama in the 1960s had to ride in the back of the bus and use segregated toilets; just as the youth of Valle de Bravo, Mexico cannot aspire to one day stand hand in hand with the children of those who drive in for the weekend in their German sports cars; so too, England in 1914 was not open to the sons of coal miners, regardless of how well they had done at one of the two most prestigious universities in the country. Richard was not accepted by British "Society" and found that the best appointment he could muster was that of a government administrative official in Colombo, Ceylon, now Sri Lanka.

Arriving in Ceylon, tall, athletic, somewhat dapper, he became enamored of the second daughter of an old Ceylonese tea planting family, the Dumonteil Lagrèze, whose roots stretched back to France under Louis XIV.

Jeannine was somewhat fey as a child. Her mother, Helène, was prone to premonitions, including the almost hysterical premonition that saved the lives of her children. In 1942, the Japanese were moving their fleet to take Ceylon. The European community was mobilized for evacuation, and two vessels, the *Yorkshire* and the *Duchess of York* were commandeered to take the families from Ceylon to England. She and the children were scheduled to travel on the *Yorkshire* on April 2. The night before departure date, Helène had a premonition that disaster would befall the *Yorkshire*, and persuaded her husband to let them travel on the later departure, which they did. Some weeks later they discovered that the *Yorkshire* had been torpedoed and sunk as she and her convoy had entered the Bay of Biscay. Jeannine inherited some of this contact with the supra-natural. Days before news of her mother's death reached us, Jeannine began feeling uncomfortable, talking about lightning strikes and troubles for her mother. She knew that her mother had died days before the news reached us.

I imagine that Jeannine's feyness, her contact with the supra-natural, was a result of her somewhat secluded, lonely childhood. Fey people are close to Nature, close to the Gods that live with and around us. Her brothers were both athletes and outdoorsmen. St. John captained his school rugby team, and Max (of whom more later) was a dyslexic, poor student whose preference was to hang around with the locals and hunt buffalo or other dangerous large animals. He caused great consternation when, at age 16, he disappeared for four days, only to return with the horns of a huge buffalo that he had shot high in the Ceylonese hills.

Jeannine, by contrast, was an avid reader, a romantic, one drawn to poetry and the exotic. From her Ceylonese childhood, she was intimate with all Kipling's Just So Stories together with their fantastic and evocative illustrations. How the Leopard got his Spots; How the Camel got his Hump; and The Elephant's Child. We read these over and over from the little blue hardbound, 1951 edition from Macmillan & Co. that still graces my library. She memorized great tracts of Coleridge's Ancient Mariner and his opium induced poem Kubla Khan, reciting these at odd times when we were alone and resting, captivating us with Coleridge's immortal verse, pronounced with appropriately graphic acting:

"In Xanadu did Kubla Khan
A stately pleasure dome decree;
Where Alph, the sacred river, ran
Through caverns measureless to man
Down to a sunless sea."

Or, in her more tranquil moods, Wordsworth as he walked alone:

I wandered lonely as a cloud
That floats on high o'er vales and hills,
When all at once I saw a crowd,

A host, of golden daffodils;
Beside the lake, beneath the trees,
Fluttering and dancing in the breeze.

I remember she had an unusual phrasing, pausing after lonely, and then letting the full phrase of "the cloud that floats" run together. As though loneliness were her condition, and the sensation of floating as a cloud was a form of being transported. How could we fail to be mesmerized?

She read Mallory and Chaucer, and loved the knights and damsels. She read Kahlil Gilbran and Shelley, and was moved by the poetry. But, above all, she loved the Arabian Nights and the writers and poets of the Indian and Arabian subcontinents. These were the tales she read to us in the evening, the poems she recited until they were like family prayers.

One of her favorites was:

Awake! for Morning in the Bowl of Night
Has flung the Stone that sets the Stars to Flight.
And Lo! the Hunter of the East has caught
The Sultan's Turret in a Noose of Light

For many years when we were young, Jeannine would awaken Caitlín and me with this quatrain. It is from the Rubaiyat of Omar Khayyám, a Persian scholar, astrologer, mathematician and poet, born in 1027, almost a thousand years ago, when England was still a fiefdom of King Canute of Sweden and that band of Norman warriors had not yet crossed the English Channel to defeat a rag tag army of Saxon peasants in the battle of Hastings.

The quatrain of Wakening is also one of my favorites. I love the image of the sky being a dark bowl in which the stars are resting, and above which our earth is mysteriously suspended. I am enchanted by the image of Morning looking over the edge of the bowl and casting the stone that set the stars to flight. Finally, the Hunter from the East, the Sun, rides up with his lasso and captures the turret of the Sultan's palace in his noose, the first shaft of light catching the highest building in the town. And then, says Khayyam, the cock crows.

It is an image of hope, an image so gentle and pastoral, that it always stayed with me. It is an image I was privileged to experience some 50 years later as I walked with nomads and their camels through the Ennedi region of the Sahara desert.

Alan

Alan was born in 1923, in Macau, part of mainland China across the bay from Hong Kong where Barclay was serving as attorney general. Like most colonial children at that time, Alan was sent away to boarding school in England at the tender age of six, wearing a tie and short pants. His "home" for the next 12 years was Ampleforth College, a private, all boys, Catholic school in Northern Yorkshire. Ampleforth was formed in 1802 by Benedictine monks who still, in the 1930's, comprised most of the teachers, and imposed a strict religious discipline on the students. When Barclay was posted to Baghdad in 1931, Nuala persuaded Barclay that the boys would learn more from a year in the heart of the ancient Persia – Mesopotamia, Sumer, Babylon, Assyria, the cradle of civilization – than cooped up in another Yorkshire winter, and pulled the boys out of school for a year. The part of Persian culture that Alan grasped best was the Persians' ability with horses. He and John each had ponies and rode everywhere. They learned to play polo, to ride bareback, and to pluck a handkerchief off a bottle while cantering past. They learned dressage and show jumping. With few friends of their own age, they hung out with the Iraqi grooms or listened impatiently while the adults told them to be "seen and not heard." In 1932, the fun stopped and they were sent back to Ampleforth. John was an artist and a rebel. Alan was studious and diligent. John was expelled after he was found climbing the spires of the monastery at night, and sketching drawings of gargoyles on the abbey roof. Alan became Head of House. John joined the Royal Air Force and died in action in a "dog-fight" with German Messerchmitts over the Mediterranean. Alan was admitted to Oxford University, completed his degree in three years, joined the Irish Guards and saw action in Flanders at the end of the war when he participated in the liberation of France and Belgium. The only memory of the war that he shared with me was how welcoming the Belgian farm girls were when the British troops liberated them from the Germans.

One of Alan's phrases, used often with me, was: "In the theatre of life, there is no rehearsal." He certainly lived his life as though it was not a rehearsal, and when he died of the cancer that had gradually spread from his prostrate to his lungs since he rejected the advice of Dr. Duff to remove the prostrate (because of the reduced quality of life that would result), unlike Dylan Thomas, he didn't "rage against the dying of the light." He was ready for the final curtain and comfortable with the performance.

He was an energetic man who loved to sail and fish and ride, and was good at all of them. He also had a vibrantly curious mind. He played with ideas. He played with words. He created crossword puzzles and invented word games, geography games, history quiz-zes and on and on, so that Caitlín and I would be entertained and challenged. He had a knack for limericks and doggerel, which he composed spontaneously. Here is a ditty from a 1950 newspaper clipping announcing the bi-monthly Catholic Cathedral Building Fundraiser, known as the Fete:

> *Are you an Earl*
> *Or a Gaiety Girl?*
> *Do you rise early or late?*
> *Be you vermin in ermine*
> *Or stinking in mink*
> *You're sure to have fun at the Fete.*

His mind was always exploring, not solely in an academic way, more often in a playful way. An example: At a dinner one evening in the early '70s, he offered the provocative idea that Picasso was the reincarnation of Shakespeare. The idea was based on a play on words: Pic-as-haut, in Basque, means a spear held on high. Picasso … Shakespeare. From this pun or coincidence, Alan floated the idea, no doubt purely as an entertaining thought for dinner con-versation, that there were similarities in the works of the two great artists. His friend, Nira, challenged him to develop the idea and to present it to the Readers' Circle, a group of individuals who en-joyed literature and the arts. Alan researched and read; he played with facts and stretched the truth; and on the appointed day, with a level of seriousness, he presented the proposition that Picasso was the reincarnation of Shakespeare, as evidenced by their works. It was not until near the end of the presentation that this group of solemn solicitors, matronly mothers and eagerly aspiring nouveau intellec-tuals understood that the whole event was a spoof. It was warmly applauded and much enjoyed.

TANGANYIKA: EARLY HISTORY

Tanganyika shares a five hundred mile border with Kenya, but could hardly be more different. Before the European colonization of Africa, Tanganyika was controlled by the Arab Sultan Bargash. His main source of power and wealth was trading in slaves, most of whom were brought to the coast from an area far inland, what is now Lake Tanganyika. While English and German explorers travelled widely through Tanganyika, many in search of the source of the Nile, Tanganyika was a kind of red headed stepchild in the Scramble for Africa between 1830 and 1880.

In the early 1880's, the Sultan, hoping to find a powerful pro-tector for his position, offered parts of Tanganyika to the British and the Germans, but it was not until a German adventurer, Karl Peters, took it upon himself to negotiate "treaties" with local chief-tains, in which large tracts of land were supposedly sold for trinkets, that the European powers took note. In the Heligoland Treaty of July 1, 1890, the British and Germans cavalierly carved up Eastern Africa, drawing a line straight from the east of Lake Victoria to a point on the coast opposite the island of Pemba. In an amazing act of arrogance, however, the line was altered because Queen Victoria insisted that her grandson, the German Kaiser Wilhelm II, be given a mountain in Africa. Britain had two, Germany had none. So the border from Lake Victoria to the coast has a kink in it, putting Mt. Kilimanjaro in German East Africa.

After the First World War, Tanganyika was taken from Germany by the League of Nations, and Britain agreed to rule the territory under a "Mandate" from the League. But Tanganyika never captured the British imagination the way that Kenya did. Few were the European settlers who moved to Tanganyika, and even fewer were those who were English. Most were German; some were Dutch or Dutch Boers from South Africa. A 1931 census established the population of Tanganyika at a little over five million, of which some 8,000 were Europeans. This, in a country that is bigger than France and Germany combined.

DAR ES SALAAM

Dar es Salaam was the capital of Tanganyika, and is now the capital of Tanzania. In Arabic, Dar es Salaam means Haven of Peace, and, by contrast with the bubbling turmoil of Kenya, it was just that.

With a population of fewer than 125,000 in the mid 1950s, Dar es Salaam had that changeless quality that one feels by the Indian Ocean. The breezes started each day at mid morning, the advent of rain was entirely predictable with the seasons, and the opportunity for change, advancement, ambition, was non-existent. We lived by the ocean, a rocky path leading from the house to an iron ladder which descended through a hole in the rock wall that faced the ocean, to a grotto which filled up with crashing waves at high tide, but which was the most peaceful web of tide pools when the tide ebbed low. At a very early age, 7 or 8 years old, I would spend unsupervised hours on hands and knees crawling around the corral-ridged pools, exploring their secrets. Tiny blennies darting like flashes of silver lightning, hermit crabs emerging from cavernous holes, some sheltered by a little conical shell, others lumbering under much weightier homes. A decade later, when I first encountered the nomadic Rendille people in the desert around Lake Turkana in northern Kenya, people who carried their worldly possessions on their camels, everything from pots and pans to sheepskin houses framed around carefully calibrated branches of acacia trees, I thought of these hermit crabs. A favourite game was to gather a half dozen of these creatures, place them in the middle of a circle drawn in the sand, and bet on which would make it to the circumference first.

Often I was joined by the sons of the local fishermen who were stalking these pools for larger prey, an angelfish, an eel, or even a lobster caught in a pool by the receding tide. As we popped the little air-filled bubbles of seaweed, like bubble wrap packing material, or searched for perfect cowrie shells, they also taught me what was edible and what was dangerous. Sea urchins, those billiard ball-sized creatures with a thousand painful, poisonous, hedgehoglike spikes, were a delicacy if extracted carefully from their crevices, boiled and served with lime. But if their spikes pierced your unsuspecting foot, beware. The poison was vicious and painful, a pain relieved only by tying a slice of papaya onto your sole and resting, foot up high.

The town was divided geographically between Oyster Bay, the long stretch of sand-blessed beach where we and the other Europeans lived, and Kariuko, the African settlement on the other side of the tiny central commercial area. In between lived the Indians, who served much the same role as the Jews had in the Middle Ages in Europe. They were the merchants, the traders, the shopkeepers. They were the oil that kept commerce going. With the exception of a small but industrious Greek community, the Europeans did not involve themselves in commerce. They were either sent out from Europe to run the European owned businesses (banks, maritime fleets, car dealerships, etc.) or they were diplomats. A few, a very few, owned farms and would come down from the highlands where they farmed, to spend a week or so in the metropolis. Many of these, like the wife of my uncle Max, were of German origin, descendants of the German settlers who had settled in the coffee growing land around Mount Kilimanjaro. Some others were South Africans of Dutch origin, the Boers, who had made the staggeringly dangerous and demanding trek by oxcart some 2,000 miles north from South Africa.

The Indian community played an important role and was strikingly omnipresent in commerce. All the stores (known as *dukas*), all kinds of restaurants, including numerous excellent Indian restaurants, and the daily grind of exchanging money, making small loans, and keeping the town's infrastructure oiled, were in the hands of the Indian community. Karimjee's hardware store where Alan and I would provision the yachts and dinghies with pulleys and cleats, varnish and sandpaper. Abdullah's corner grocery, where one could find any household need, but always just one of everything. There was no choice. It was either the green soap from Bombay, or no soap at all. As we tagged behind Jeannine striding through the streets of the Indian part of town, feeling the texture of the huge rolls of fabric lined up against the walls, or sniffing the spices arrayed in large baskets of various colors, we were bombarded with sounds, smells, visions of extraordinary exoticism. The crowded stores blared tunes from Bollywood movies, dance production tunes, melancholy melodies undulating from sitars and oboe-like shehnais. The narrow streets were pungent with turmeric and cumin and curry, but also fragrant with perfumes and frangipani. The sari-wrapped women, elegant and seductive, redolent of the allure of the East.

It would be a mistake to generalize about "the Indian community". In fact, the Indian community of Dar es Salaam was a fascinating pot pourri of subcultures. Probably the most prominent were the Ishmailis, a Shia Muslim sect that followed The Aga Khan. During the '50s and '60s, the Aga Khan was an elderly, very corpulent gentleman, who was weighed annually with much fanfare, and was then awarded his weight in jewels by his followers. His son, Aly Khan, was the diametric opposite of this portly, gentle man. Aly was a playboy of legendary dimension. Racehorses, diamonds, fast cars, and beautiful women were his staple. He married, among others, Rita Hayworth, the Hollywood sex symbol of the '40s. But it was still a surprise when, in 1957, the old Sultan Muhammed Shah, Aga Khan III, named his grandson Karim, a mere 20 year Harvard student, to succeed him. Karim became active in the East African Ishmaili community, contributing large amounts to hospitals and schools, and encouraging religious and racial harmony.

The Hindu community was the most colorful. Jeannine took Caitlín and me to visit the Hindu temples, crammed full with interesting Gods. She was familiar with them from her childhood: Ganesh, the elephant god; Vishnu, the sensuous dancing woman with six hands; and Brahma, the four-headed god who grew in a lotus out of the navel of the sleeping goddess Vishnu. The Hindu women flocked to the Indian market dressed in beautiful, delicate saris, a red dot marking their forehead, and often with flowers in their hair. We loved the playfulness of Hinduism, the exoticness of their temples, the beauty of the Hindu women.

The Sikhs were intimidating. Tall, statuesque, with their turbans piled high on their heads and their long, untrimmed beards combed backward and tied up with a cord or wrapped under their turban. They were descended from the most elite troops used by the British in the Indian army, and their presence still commanded respect. Many Sikhs served as policemen, or men in authority in some civil service role. The Sikh religion is monotheistic, and much less interesting to the mind of young children. However, we were invited to the opening of the new Sikh Temple in 1962, no doubt because of Alan's position with the newspaper. The Sikhs exuded discipline, and held no charm for us.

Finally, rounding out the religious pot were Goans, a small group of Catholics, from the tiny province of Goa on the Western shore of India, once ruled and converted by fervently religious Portuguese settlers. One Goan family adopted Jeannine, insisting she sit down for tea and sweet biscuits in their hardware store whenever she visited. They had lived for some years in Pondicherry, a town in southern India that had been colonized by the French, and they loved to practice their pigeon French with her.

Each community had its temples, its mosques, its churches, and although we were Catholics, our parents made a point of taking us to visit them, to meet their imams and gurus, in an effort to open our minds to the wondrous multifaceted nature of the world's religions.

The language of most of the coast of Eastern Africa, from Somalia south through Kenya and Tanzania, all the way to the northern part of Mozambique, is Kiswahili, a Bantu language heavily salted with Arabic. The Arabic influence comes from over 1000 years of Arab presence the breadth and width of the Indian Ocean. During the late

1800s in particular, the Sultan of Oman ruled great swaths of this East African coast, including the evocative island of Zanzibar, home of a dozen exotic spices: cloves, coriander, cardamom, cinnamon, ginger, vanilla sticks, lemon grass, nutmeg and others. The Omanis plied their trade sailing their majestic dhows north from India to the shores of the Saudi and Omani deserts, and south past Lamu and Mombasa, on the Kenya coast, to Zanzibar, and on to Bagamoyo and Dar es Salaam on the Tanzanian coast, even on to Mozambique and Madagascar. In the months of December and January they sailed south with a north-westerly breeze filling their lateen rigged sails, returning after the summer monsoons of July and August, as the winds shifted back to the south. In addition to trading cloves and spices, the Arabs traded gold, ivory and rhino horns from the interior of Africa. But, more lucrative than any of these in the 19th century was the trade in slaves. The Arab traders ventured deep inland, almost to the Congo, exchanging guns, beads and cloth for humans, who they then force-marched back to the coast, typically to the ports of Kilwa and Bagamoyo, for shipment to the palaces of Oman and Saudi and even India.

BAGAMOYO

Jeannine loved Bagamoyo. She would often take me and Caitlín the 75 kilometers or so, a three-hour drive, up the coast from Dar es Salaam to visit. Its old buildings were haunted by the souls of slaves, singing melancholy dirges as they were led away, chains at their ankles, and shackled by their wrists to the long mangrove tree trunks that kept them progressing in single file.

From a very early age, Bagamoyo evoked a strong emotional response in me. Bagamoyo was the place from which many of the great explorers, Burton, Speke, and Stanley, my earliest heroes, set out in search of the source of the Nile and on other romantic explorations. I was also intrigued by a darker part of its history. Bagamoyo means: "I lay down my heart". Not only was it the place from which white explorers started their journey inland, it was also the place from which black slaves were shipped to Zanzibar from where Arab traders sent them on to the palaces of Oman, and to the slave markets of the Saudi peninsular. I imagined row upon row of powerful, black men, chained together, singing sad songs of their local villages, their wives and children, as they were auctioned off and led away. I felt the ghosts of these men, and even as a small boy I wondered how man can treat man in such a way, like goods or cattle for trading and profit.

Bagamoyo is now, and was then, home to an age-old tradition of woodworking. For the most part this involves dhow building. Men dressed in *kikois* (essentially loin cloths) sit cross-legged as they carve each spar, each beam of these magnificent vessels, heirs to over three hundred years of sailing prowess. Around them run little children, naked, playing in the sand and waves, silhouetted against a backdrop of crumbling stone buildings, built at a time when over 50,000 slaves a year passed through the town, many of them being auctioned off in the town square. But there is also a tradition of finer wood carving and over the years Jeannine had befriended, and commissioned works from some of the more artistic wood carvers. During the summer of 1960, the summer before Caitlín and I were shipped off to Europe to school, we visited Bagamoyo on one of Jeannine's wood carver trips. As we walked the sandy footpaths between huts made from the fronds of coconut trees and the branches of the baobab, we encountered two old men playing Bao. This is an ancient game involving the placement of baobab seeds in lines of indentations carved into a heavy wooden beam. It is a mathematical game in which my seeds can "eat" your seeds (they use the word *kula*, to eat, although a better description might be to capture, since your seeds become mine and fight on my side) if they land in the indentation in front of an encampment of your seeds. It is played at a frightening speed, somewhat like the way the Chinese play Mah Jong or dominoes, with the hands dipping into the bag of seeds, dropping them in an indentation on my side, and then rapidly spreading them around the board. I was fascinated and insisted that I be permitted to stay and watch until I understood the rules. So Jeannine wandered off to engage her old woodworker in conversation. Caitlín, trotting beside her, in flip flops, pony tail and wide bright eyes, her olive skin glistening, attracted the children of the village, and before long she was teaching them all hop scotch in the sand with stones and the seeds of palm trees.

Little did we know, Jeannine was on a mission. She returned to Bagamoyo many times that summer and autumn, for she had commissioned two works, one for Caitlín and one for me, as gifts for when we returned to Africa the following year. For Caitlín she designed a Christmas crib, but instead of the traditional cow and sheep, she had zebra and giraffe, warthogs and impala beside the crib. The manger was laid in a traditional African hut, and the visitors carried drums and spears. Caitlín still has this crib. For me she commissioned an exquisite chess set. The pawns are drummers, their djembe between their bended knees. The castle a hut, the king and queen the patriarchal and matriarchal figures of a traditional Swahili household, and, best of all, the knights were elephants with elegant trunks and tusks made from the sun-dried spines of tiny fish. When I left Kenya for America I forgot this chess set, but Jeannine kept it as she travelled from Dar es Salaam to Nairobi to London and back to Karen. I retrieved it some 50 years later.

BUNDUKI

My earliest memories of my father are of fishing trips in very early childhood. Our outings to the Bunduki fishing camp were among the family's favorite excursions. The car was packed full on Friday night. Sleeping bags, woolen underwear, rain jackets, and food for the weekend. Also rods, line, flies, nets, waders, swimsuits and so on. Long before dawn we were bundled into the car. In the Uluguru mountains, some three hours drive from Dar es Salaam, the trout would feed for the first and last couple of hours of the day, but the rest of the day they searched for the cool, deep waters, avoiding the heat of the sun. As dawn broke we were driving up a rutted mountain trail and parking by a rickety wooden footbridge across which we carried the weekend's provisions. By sun up Alan is on the river, casting to the heads of the riffles, watching, hawk-eyed, his fly drifting downstream until that electric moment when a fish rises to the fly, his rod bends, the dance of the tight line, the flash of rainbow as the trout makes a dash for the fast water, trying to find the strength to break free; and ultimately the gentle, almost caressing way in which he holds the trout, still underwater, as he carefully releases the fly, softly holds the trout in his hands, mouth upstream, and, after a pause in which the trout seems to be catching its breath, it darts away and returns to its pool.

I loved to be with him as he played the trout, but often, as he cast and gathered line, I would wander off and explore. Here come Jeannine and Caitlín.

"You want to play pooh sticks, Jules?" Caitlín asks. We head downstream to some faster water where Alan won't be fishing. The three of us chose a stick and hand it to Jeannine.

"Mine is the straight one like a sailboat," I proclaim.

"And mine has a Y so it goes faster in the calm water," says Caitlín.

"First one to the bridge wins," announces Jeannine as she drops the three sticks in the river. Caitlín and I hurry along the river's edge, avoiding overhanging trees and awkwardly positioned boulders as we go, watching our sticks intently, hoping they will not get hung up on a rock or a side pool.

"I won, I won," cries Caitlín jumping up and down on the bridge, but I am already distracted. In the pool below the bridge I catch sight of a Malachite Kingfisher, his tail down and beak in the air as he sits astride a branch hanging over the pool. His head and back are a brilliant dark blue, with a tuft of black hairs, his beak a vibrant orange and his legs are red. Suddenly he swings over and dives head first into the river, emerging with a fingerling trout in his beak. His wings flapping furiously, like those of a hummingbird, so fast they are merely a whirl of color, he whacks the unfortunate trout's head against a stone, flips it in the air, and swallows it head first.

Caitlín and Jeannine head down the path a ways, and I grab my butterfly net, intent on catching an interesting specimen. As they lie in the high grass, watching the grasshoppers leap from stalk to stalk, I spy a Citrus Swallowtail perched on a twig. Its wings are grey black splashed with white, like paint thrown against an aging barn door. On his lower back, looking at me are two "eyes", not the eyes he sees with, which are large, round and black, but his beautiful decorative marking, bright blue eyes with a flame of red and a dab of white below. After a few futile swipes I catch him resting on the ground and pounce with my net. Once entrapped, I nudge him into my empty jam jar in which there lies a swab of cotton wool soaked in nail polish. Soon he is anaesthetized and I run back to Jeannine and Caitlín to show them my latest specimen.

"Wow, how beautiful" exclaims Caitlín. Jeannine, reverting to Wordsworth and her poetic mood, recites:

"I've watched you now full half an hour
Self poised upon that yellow flower."

I join them, lying back, relaxed with my conquest. Jeannine is silent. Caitlín points out a dragon in the sky, white and fluffy, blowing smoke at a castle, which morphs into a knight and retaliates. A sunbird flitters by, on its way to suck the pollen out of some welcoming flower. After a while Caitlín and I also fall silent, and Jeannine says:

"Let's play the game, the butterfly game."

We close our eyes and concentrate on listening. At first all we hear is the river gurgling by. As with the strings in an orchestra, the river's gurgle is made up of a variety of tones, the brittle sound of fast water rippling over small rocks and pebbles, the deeper sound as a pool forms behind a larger rock, the occasional splash as a trout emerges to sip a fly from the surface. The gurgle becomes background, like the sound of traffic in a city. It is now a mood, a theme, an atmosphere. Then a bird sings, and is answered. It is amazing how birds sing. Often one bird has several different calls, and although they are repeated, they are not always repeated in the same order. A warbler calls and another responds. At first an echo, and then a complimentary tune. We start to hear and recognize the birdcalls, the flutes and clarinets of the concerto. A bee buzzes by and alights on a flower. A small branch falls, a monkey chatters in the distance. I am woken from my eyes-closed concentration by the feel of something alighting on my elbow, a dragonfly, his long blue abdomen hanging from his gossamer wings like man's first engine of flight, the Kitty Hawk. A butterfly rests on my knee. We call the game Listening to Butterflies, the game in which you try to keep excluding the louder sounds and sights until, in the end, if there is ever an end, the most insignificant sound becomes an instrument.

Alan inspired me to be adventurous. Jeannine instilled in us a love of Nature.

For Caitlín and me, Bunduki was our own extended enchanted garden. We knew its pools and waterfalls, its rocks and bridges as though they were our backyard. The path from the cabin, where Caitlín, aged six, would bathe in a large cooking pot, lead down to a waterfall that thundered into a large pool. We never caught fish here, though fish there must have been. Instead, we spent hours jumping from rocks into the spray, swimming against the current to see how close we could get to the torrent of falling water, and counting the skips of a stone skimmed across the pool. From the large pool the stream turned right and ran down some hundred yards of riffles, under the rickety wooden bridge and into another, quieter, deep, left-turning pool that dug in under overhanging banks and bushes. From there another straight stretch that was crossed by the more substantial bridge on which the entire Catholic population of Bunduki would cross to the church on the hill, dressed in head scarfs, *kikois* and shawls of fantastic colors and designs, like so many pineapples lining up on the dusty path.

Caitlín was the prettiest, most effervescent little girl, always with a friend, the antithesis of her bookish elder brother. When left to my own devices, which was often, I would either engross myself in an adventure novel (King Solomon's Mines, Prester John, etc.), explore for frogs and insects, or join the African children hanging out around their mothers, gathering fruit, pushing tire rims with a stick, or otherwise inventing activities. Later, in my early teens, I was brave enough to invite friends. One such friend was John Cashin. At 17 he was three years older than me, large, almost giant, unathletic and serious. If he were 17 today, he would be seated behind a computer hacking some high-level security site. We invented word games, created crossword puzzles and wrote clues in the style of The Times crosswords. We tended to telegraph the clue, but thought we were being very cryptic. *"Police roundup leaves tea at end of muddied garden."* I pose. *"Dragnet"* says John. For those who never spent hours deciphering The Times crossword, a word like *muddied* might indicate an anagram. So, *garden* reconfigured, with a T at the end, produces *dragnet*, a police roundup.

As the years passed, I learned how to read a river. Where the fish lie and why. How the banks provide protection from hawks and ospreys that would swoop down and capture them in their long claws, and how these same banks offer the fish the opportunity to catch a grasshopper or bug that falls carelessly in the stream. How the eddies downstream of a large rock create a dip in the riverbed behind the rock in which a fish could lie, at rest, without having to fight the current, ready to dart out to snatch a drowned nymph or even an emerging fly that was spreading its wings as it rests for seconds on the surface of the water, ready to take its first flight. How the natural flies drift or swim or struggle to the surface, and how our imitation flies need to mirror this movement, or else the fish will not be interested.

Gradually I grew to appreciate that the true joy of fly fishing lies not in catching the fish, but in everything that goes before: being in the stream and feeling its force against one's legs; watching the ducks, the geese, the beavers, and yes the deer and smaller mammals as they approach the water shyly, hesitantly, wary of the presence of other beings; reading the water to understand how the fish are lying; watching flies emerge from the river, studying them, matching the fly on your line to the fly on the river; presenting the fly without a ripple, without any drag in the water so that a careful fish is not spooked; managing your line so that you are in constant contact, visual or tactile, with your fly, so that not only can you feel the strike of the fish, but you can anticipate it. Catching and landing a fish is exhilarating, and releasing it has much of the same tenderness as post coital relaxation.

If you spend half a day in the river and never see a fish, it is still a fine day.

A RING OF ISLANDS
In addition to its mosaic of races and cultures that became second nature to me and Caitlín, Dar es Salaam also boasted an excellent harbor. Shaped like a bagpipe, or the spleen of a goat, the harbor was a large round basin, open to the ocean by only the narrowest of channels. And beyond that channel, a ring of islands some three miles out, dotting the coastline and providing a reef barrier that, supposedly, discouraged sharks from entering. These islands were our weekend retreats. Closest to the harbor are Honeymoon Island

and Sinda Island. Further north are Bongoyo and Mbudya. Every weekend the (primarily European) sailing community sailed out to the islands to anchor, snorkel, walk the pristine beaches, sip on gin and tonics, and then return with a following wind and a setting sun. Simple pleasures entertained us. Caitlín and Angela jump off the foredeck into inner tubes, peeling tangerines and counting the seeds to see who has the most. I dive in with my goggles to see what fish and corral I find. Although this is open ocean, the principal dangers are a scrape on the corral, the sting of a small stingray, or the searing pain from the poison of a sea urchin's spine, whose swelling is cured by tying a paw-paw (*papaya*) to the entry point of the spine permitting the papain enzyme to work as a meat tenderizer breaking down the urchin's spine. After lunch Jeannine admonishes us: "No swimming for an hour after lunch. You could get cramps and drown. Sit quietly and read." Possibly, this is her way of ensuring that the "grown-ups" can take a nap without having to keep an eye on the children. When the hour is up we plunge back in the water, race to the beach and build moated sand castles where we imprison hermit crabs and bet on which will escape first. In the evening, as the sun sets behind the island, we sail west with the wind behind us. Alan asks Jeannine to sit on the boom because the "kicking strap" (whose job is to restrain the boom from riding up and to keep the sail's shape for maximum thrust) is not working. One evening, as she is sitting there, looking back over the boat's transom at shafts of sunlight setting on a dark blue sea, the wind shifts, catches the back of the sail, and sends sail, boom and Jeannine flying to the other side, catapulting her into an ignominious dunking in the ocean.

CHAPTER 5

OF SCHOOLBOYS AND OTHER ANIMALS

BOARDING SCHOOL

At six years old I was sent off to Soni, an all-boys boarding school on the foothills of Kilimanjaro. "Sent off" sounds like a punishment. Nothing could have been further from the truth. My few friends were all older than me, and most of them had already left for school. I was eager to leave home. But eagerness does not always overcome one's more basic instincts. My first days at Soni tapped deeply into my, and others', basic animal instincts.

It was a full day drive by bus from Dar to Soni. We arrived a little after dark to the village of Soni, some three miles from the school. The village had one road, a muddy track, fit for Land Rovers and other hardy vehicles. It had a tin roofed storehouse selling maize and coffee, but not much else. It had a one-room schoolhouse and a few shebeens where men could spend their earnings on drink and on a handful of women who had given up on life. At seven at night, a few lights were coming on in the larger homes, beer was flowing in the shebeens, a couple of families were scurrying home, but the roads and the village itself were dark. The school bus disembarked and everyone piled into smaller VW mini-buses to transport them the last three miles up into the mountains to St. Michael's School at Soni. All, it transpired, except myself. As the youngest, least experienced, I had missed the opportunity to jump on the mini bus, and was left standing in front of the large bus waiting for someone to pick me up. At that moment a very portly German woman, Frau Richter, appeared in her dilapidated VW bug, and told me to jump in for the ride to school. It started to rain. Mud formed in the road. The VW's lights barely pierced the darkness as we slid from side to side of the road. It was just myself and Frau Richter after a long day's journey, and I felt lonely and afraid. This was a very dark place, with a completely unknown, intimidatingly large, barely English-speaking woman who claimed to be taking me to the school.

Eventually we arrived. The impressive feature of the school was its dormitory. All the boys, I estimate about 160, aged six to ten years old, were housed in two long, contiguous buildings, in which two rows of beds reached from the central "control center", where the two dormitory priests resided, to the limit of each long room. About eighty beds in each dormitory; forty on each side. Frau Richter left me at the front of the dormitory, and with a rather oppressive, and distinctly too blousy hug, wished me well. I picked up my little suitcase, not much bigger than a lunch box, and entered. I was directed to turn right and find my bed. I was the last boy to arrive, and as I walked up the dormitory, past the rows and rows of beds, I felt all the eyes watching me. "He's the new boy" I heard. "What's his name?" No one said hello, or welcomed me or directed me. Even those boys I knew said little, and barely acknowledged me. I kept walking until I reached the last bed, next to Fatty Hartmann, who told me that the final bed was mine. I had walked past eighty pairs of eyes without anyone addressing me, and felt very alone for the first time in my life. That night, after I had uncurled my mosquito net, taken my toothbrush and paste out of the little satchel and walked back to the central bathroom by the control center, past 80 pairs of eyes, to brush my teeth and pee, and returned again, still without recognition, I tucked into bed and fell asleep. But the ordeal had not ended. That night, and it was to be the last night that this ever happened, I pee'd in my bed and vomited on my mosquito net. I wanted more than anything to be home with my mother. I had not known fear, but it is primal when thrown into unknown surroundings. So began boarding school life.

The next lesson in basic instincts came about a week later. A group of us were playing on the open fields in front of the dining hall. For some reason lost now in the fog of memory, a fight began, and I was thrown in. As the fighting progressed, some of the younger boys took the opportunity to pin me to the ground and deliver a few blows. In an almost systematic fashion, boys of ever diminishing social hierarchy followed suit, until even the smallest, youngest boys took a shot. This did not stop until, finally, in a rage of fear and anger, I was able to better one poor boy, and establish my ranking among this animal kingdom. Robert Ardrey's *Territorial Imperative* was at play, and I learned, although only subconsciously, about alpha males and social dominance.

The third experience with basic instincts occurred some two years later. Fatty Hartmann and I still had beds side by side as older boys left and our position in the dormitory rose. One morning, while everyone else was at Mass, the first activity of the day, we slipped under our beds with the intention of completing homework that we had not finished the night before. As we scribbled and muttered, Father Collins, the dormitory monitor, heard us and discovered us under the beds. This was an infraction, and would, no doubt be punished. He told us he would talk with us later.

Father Collins was in his early thirties. An ascetic man, who ate little, exercised a lot, and maintained himself in excellent physical condition. He had arrived from England at the beginning of the school year and was placed in charge of the boys aged eight to ten. He was a fierce disciplinarian, and held us all in fear, so it was with much trepidation that we awaited his call for us to visit with him in his room. It was not until I began to write this book that I discovered all I now know about him, but I remember vividly the next sequence of events.

About 2.00 a.m. the night after the skipping Mass incident, I was awakened by Father Collins who told me to follow him to his room. After speaking a little about the importance of attending Mass daily and conforming with the rules, he asked me whether Fatty Hartmann and I were touching each other's private parts. I said No. He then asked about other boys. Did I touch other boys' private parts? Did I know if other boys were touching each other? And the conversation, or rather, the interrogation went on like this for about 30 minutes. At the end he warned me not to talk about these things because they were very evil and it was his job to know what was going on in the dormitory. Although he made no attempt to molest me, I was keenly aware that this was not a comfortable situation, and did all I could from then on to stay out of his way.

As I worked on researching this book, I googled Soni School expecting to be reminded of the long hikes into the hills, the waterfalls, the camaraderie. Instead I discovered that a group of boys of my generation, and younger, had brought suit against the Rosminian Order of Catholic priests who ran the school and another school in England called Grace Dieu, alleging that they had been systematically abused over a long period of time by this very Father Collins and at least three other priests. Father Collins, it transpired, had been exposed as a pedophile at Grace Dieu and had been sent out to Tanganyika where no one would know about his predilections. A BBC television program, *"Abuse: Breaking the Silence"*, was aired in March 2011. Grown men, some of whom I had known quite well at Soni, cried as they recounted their tales of this dreadful perverted man. It was shocking, appalling, and quite chilling to realize how close I had come to evil, to another basic instinct, and I thank my good stars for the narrow escape.

EXPERIENCES WITH ANIMALS

I was a voracious reader as a child. My favourite books were books about living in the wild, living with animals, and exploration. One of the writers who first captured my mind was Gerald Durrell, the author of *My Family and Other Animals*. Gerald Durrell grew up in an eccentric, single mother family on the island of Corfu, and, as the youngest of four children, he was often left to his own resources. While his eldest brother, Lawrence Durrell, author of *The Alexandria Quartet*, patronized the family with his sarcastic and sardonic wit, and his sister, Margo, either "trailing muslin and scent" or sunbathing in the olive groves in a microscopic swimsuit "collected an ardent band of handsome peasant youths", Gerry wandered the olive-rich landscape with Roger, his dog. Durrell, at 12 and 13, discovered the magic of trapdoor spiders, of chameleonlike rose beetles that adapted their hue to that of the rose on whose petals they rested, and of sea slugs and hermit crabs in tide pools on the Corfu shore.

Like Gerald Durrell, I grew up with animals. My pets included tortoises, bush babies and even, for a few days, a baby buffalo. But wild animals are not best as pets. They are best in their natural environment, contributing in their special way to the complex and intricate web that is Nature. My uncle Max, Jeannine's younger brother, was the first game warden of Manyara National Park, a jewel nestled close to Olduvai, in the shadow of Mount Kilimanjaro. He had graduated from Ceylonese tea planter, to well respected naturalist, zoologist and conservationist. In the 1950's work was just beginning on the tracking of animals, in particular on the tracking of the great herds of plains game that moved north and south through the Serengeti during the migrations. Michael Grzimek (author of *Serengeti Shall Not Die)* and a handful of others including Max, captured wildebeest and painted their horns different colors so that they could be individually recognised from the air from within the herds that seasonally moved in and out of Manyara Park.

When I was eight, Max invited my father and me to accompany him on one of these painting expeditions. He had an old, open bed Land Rover. The driver and I in front. Max, my father and a ranger in the back. Max had rigged up a lasso attached to a long branch of something reminiscent of bamboo. He instructed the driver to head out in search of wildebeest herds and then to plunge in to the midst of the thickest herd. It was the wildest ride. We were not on an airport landing strip, but in the middle of the East African plains, and every termite mound, every foxhole, shook the car to its bones. The wildebeest cared less as they galloped helter-skelter away from our vehicle. Finally we were able to get close enough for Max to drop the lasso noose over the head of a mature male wildebeest. Instantly my father and the ranger leapt out of the back, the car bouncing to a halt, and wrestled the struggling beast to the ground. Max, having secured the lasso, jabbed an enormous syringe into the rear quarters of the terrified animal. A tranquilizer. As soon as the wildebeest was calm, they set about inserting a tag into its ears and painting one horn red and one horn blue. Later, as the drugged animal stumbled to his feet and hesitatingly trotted off to join the remainder of the herd, who snorted in puzzlement as this coloured member of the species joined them, I felt saddened. Wildebeests are supremely ugly animals. They have scruffy beards. Their manes are unkempt and straggly. Although they are the size of a horse, they are in fact antelopes, and their build is ungainly and uneven. They have none of the majesty of a horse, nor any of the beauty of the smaller antelopes, gazelles, impala and so on. Yet, I was able to touch this wildebeest as he lay drugged and panting beside the Land Rover. Watching him leave, I felt the loss of a friend. Animals, including wild animals, were friends for us in those early days. Today the path of the Serengeti migration is well known, but in those days it was still uncharted territory, and these primitive painting expeditions were the first step in the process of documenting the movement of the great herds.

On one trip to visit uncle Max we came across a dead buffalo, already torn apart by hyena. Max said she was a female who had recently given birth and was still feeding her young. So we spent the better part of the morning looking for traces of the young buffalo, fearing that it too would fall prey to hyenas. We were lucky, and found the calf curled up, nestled in some high grass near an anthill. Max and one of his rangers were able to corral the infant and to tie it down in the back of the Land Rover. That night the baby buffalo slept in the back area of Max's house. We would visit every day and feed it with a baby's milk bottle, the buffalo wrapping its large lips around the teat of the bottle and sucking energetically.

A couple of days later Max discovered that he was missing some sheets, and demanded an explanation from his housekeeper. When no explanation was forthcoming Max did what he did so well in the wild. He looked for animal tracks, and to our surprise, discovered the marks of a dragged object, and then some shreds of sheet pinned to a prickly bush nearby. Determined to discover what had happened, and who was the culprit, Max rigged up a string across a ground level window, left the window slightly open and tied a bell to the string. He then placed some rugs on the floor near the window, and went to sleep with a flashlight and a revolver by his head. About one in the morning he heard the bell tinkle, grabbed his flashlight and shone it at the pair of small lights he saw ahead of him, the eyes of the intruder. To his surprise, he found himself face to face with a large leopard, standing, or rather crouching, a yard or two from the foot of his bed. Keeping the flashlight steadily fixed on the leopard's face with his left hand, he gradually reached across his chest with his right hand and found his revolver, which he also pointed at the leopard in case it decided to make a move. Instead, the leopard, even more stealthily than Max, backed slowly out the window, the way he had come in.

The next morning, as Max recounted the story and showed us the dusty footprints of the leopard by the window outside the house, he mused that maybe the leopard had been first attracted into the house by the smell of the baby buffalo in the back room, and decided that he needed to either house the buffalo elsewhere or to find some other place it could stay while it grew strong enough to be released back into the park.

That was not the last time a leopard crossed my path. A few years later, also while staying with Max, he took me, my father and mother, to shoot francolin and guinea fowl, two of the plumper, better tasting, wild birds. A warm, dry wind rippled across the tall grass, bending stalks to its will. Grasshoppers leapt in great bounds from our feet. An occasional small bird shrieked and noisily flapped its way to a nearby thorn bush. We walked single file, Max in front, myself behind, eager to feel important and close to the action, my father behind me and Jeannine at the back. Max had long legs, and walked with rapid strides like a sandpiper, effortlessly covering great expanses of ground. I trotted behind, occasionally skipping with that little stride and skip that the Maasai use when covering long distances. Suddenly, not a foot in front of me, a cobra raised its head and front body off the ground, curving backward like an S, its head facing Max and ready to strike. Max had stepped within inches of it as he passed, causing it to spring to action. Emitting a mix of gasp and shriek, I leapt backward, almost tripping over my father behind me. Max spun around, instantly saw the cobra and raised his gun to shoot. His brain working as fast as his instincts, he saw me behind the snake, realized that his shotgun would spray pellets even at such close range, and he refrained from firing. The cobra, fortunately made a similar calculation, ducked down as fast as he had risen, and sped off into the bush.

The day was yet early, and we had seen few birds, so Max led us to a dried up *wadi* or riverbed. Placing himself on one bank, and my father on the other, he instructed my mother and me to walk up the *wadi* a few yards ahead of them. The idea was that we would scare up the guinea fowl, which nest and eat on the ground, rather like quail, and they would then take off, flying up to where they were easy targets for the hunters. The *wadi* was some six to eight feet deep, quite heavily shrubbed on either side, but just short grass where we walked below. Ahead we saw a fallen tree spanning from bank to bank, some 12 feet ahead of us. At that moment, appearing out of the branches of the fallen tree on one bank a leopard stalked, with the stealth and grace of a shark appearing from behind a rock cave, its large paws softly and unerringly floating silently along the tree trunk. To me it seemed the largest, most menacing thing I had seen. It stopped in the middle of the tree, and stared at us. We froze. Its yellow eyes seemed haunted and distant, but its shoulders and haunches exuded power. We looked at each other for an eternity. Leopards are not arrogant like lions. Lions fear no one, no thing. When you come upon a lion that is dozing, which the male lions seem to do most of the time, he will probably ignore you. If you come too close, he will draw himself to full height and stare at you, his tail swinging slowly, curved up at the end, like a scythe cutting grass, until the moment that he decides to charge. Leopards, however, are more reluctant, even shy. The Maasai will tell you that they are untrustworthy, unpredictable, even devious; not brave or heroic. There was no way to know what he was thinking as he paused on the tree trunk, compact, powerful, menacing. My mother and I were at once both petrified and mesmerized. He was too far to reach us with a single leap, so why would he attack. Neither of us raised our arms or gave any indication of aggression. He padded softly on, disappearing into the bush on the other side.

As the moment passed, and we stopped to discuss whether to continue, I was more elated than fearful. Even though Jeannine had grown up close to the bush, and her brothers had both been outdoorsmen, I have no doubt that she feared for her child. But she deferred to Max, who was, after all, the game warden of the adjacent park, and lived among these creatures. She knew, however, and it was also part of the culture, that so long as fear was not countenanced, named or recognized, its power was contained. Like an evil African spirit, it could be kept at bay by being ignored.

Today it is hard to see leopards in Kenya. For a while, in the '70s and '80s they were heavily poached. Fortunately, they seem to be regaining ground in recent years. So much so that even in the Langata forest by Alan's home in Karen he encountered leopard in the weeks before his death in 2002. He was riding, as he did every day, with his dogs in the forest, when a leopard suddenly leapt out of the undergrowth and attacked one of the dogs on the trail where Alan was riding. He told me the story, three weeks later as he lay dying in the hospital of the Vatican in Rome. He said that as he locked eyes with the leopard, he saw fear. No doubt the size of horse and rider was intimidating. Alan spurred his horse, Everest, to charge the leopard, which had his dog, Mickey Finn, by the neck, but the leopard leapt briskly away carrying the wretched dog to its untimely death.

In the 1950's, when we visited Max in Manyara, the buffalo herds in Lake Manyara numbered more than 1000 head in the herd. In Tsavo National Park there were 8,000 rhino and the elephant population was over 45,000. By the late 1980s, you were lucky if you saw a herd of fifty buffalo in Manyara, the rhino were almost extinct in Tsavo, and the elephant population in that beautiful park had dropped to 6,000. The experience of being confronted by a herd of 1,200 buffalo, with the alpha males standing guard in front as you approach, is completely different from that of coming upon 10 docile buffalo grazing quietly on the plains. The guardian males raise their monstrously horned heads and sniff the air. If you are close enough you can see the wetness of their noses, the steam rising from their breath, and the occasional stamping when they feel uncomfortably close to an unwelcome stranger. Poaching in the 1970s decimated these populations. Today the landscape of some Kenya parks feels more like a drive through a zoo than the expedition of wonder and affinity that it did fifty years ago. But they are still worth visiting. Once you have felt the breeze of the savannahs permeate your skin, the endless sunsets imprint deep reds and gold on your retinae, and the sound of lion roaring behind your camp become second nature to your soul, you will never forget Africa.

TEENAGE IN TANGANYIKA

The extraordinary thing about East Africa in the early '60s is that it was a petrie dish for all kinds of scientists: Anthropologists, primatologists, palaeontologists, archaeologists and conservationists. Imagine this collection of characters that populated our remote corner of the world:

Louis and Mary Leakey, who, in 1960, discovered Paranthropus boisei, for a long time considered the oldest human specimen, and proof that human life began in the Rift Valley of Tanganyika. I was able to visit Olduvai Gorge, the site of the Leakeys' excavations in the mid '60s accompanied by my game warden uncle Max, who knew the Leakeys.

Robert Ardrey, author of *African Genesis: A Personal Investigation into the Animal Origins and Nature of Man* (1961), and *The Territorial*

Imperative (1966), both ground-breaking studies of how animals fight for territory and how that reflects on humanity.

Joy Adamson, author of *Born Free*, published 1961.

Bernard and Michael Grzimek, author and cinematographer, respectively, of the Academy Award winning documentary *Serengeti shall not Die* (1959). Michael Grzimek died when a Rupell's Griffon vulture struck the leading edge of the right wing of his single engine, zebra-striped, World War II Fieseler Stork causing the aileron rod to bend and putting the aircraft into a steep and fatal right hand dive into the ground. At the time, Grzimek was flying over the Serengeti tracking the migration of the wildebeest and other animals. Grzimek was also a friend of uncle Max and invited him to be part of this ground-breaking effort in the Serengeti.

Jane Goodall, who pioneered the study of primates in the wild and was the first to document the intelligent use of tools by chimpanzees in her book *In the Shadow of Man*. After her first husband, Hugo van Lawick, died, Jane married Derick Bryceson, then Minister of Tourism, who lived next door to us in Dar es Salaam.

When I was still a child, not yet a teenager, Durrell's writings triggered a flood of inquisitiveness, not only of animals, insects, flora and fauna, but of humanity itself. As I approached and entered my teens, these scientists, and others like Desmond Morris (author of *The Naked Ape* (1966)), inspired a fascination with the emergence of Man as a species, and what that meant for beliefs about the role of God in our lives. At that time we were practising Catholics. I had been raised with the Catholic Catechism, which – how well I remember these lines as though the nuns were with me now – started:

Q: Who made me?

A: God made me.

Q: Why did God make me?

A: God made me to know Him, love Him and serve Him in this world, and to be happy with Him for ever after in the next.

Leakey's discoveries, linking Man with ape, challenged the heart of this dogma. Goodall reinforced the sense that animals and humans shared a common thread; that, in the end, much of our behaviour is animal in its origins. Grzimek was the icing on the cake, the great, dramatic painting of an animal world so complex and interwoven as to be the source of endless investigation and discovery.

Each of these cast doubt on the dogma I had learned from the nuns in Dar es Salaam and the priests at Soni.

CHAPTER 6

THE COLONIAL IDENTITY

What is the essence of the Colonial identity? What was it that made the British colonials a breed apart, for better or for worse? What made them different from their relatives "back home", and from the similarly situated Belgian and French colonials? Clearly, the breadth and power of the British Empire far exceeded that of other countries. This gave to the British colonials a certain sense of élitism that the other countries did not enjoy. Add to that the fact that much of the Empire was ruled by men of rank and title, men (and it was all men) who felt, like Kipling that they had an obligation to "take up the White Man's burden" and send forth their best to serve the needs of the Empire. The British Colonial identity was similar to the identity of the American frontiersman in the 1820's, with an overlay of British private schooling, cut crystal decanters and afternoon tea in bone china. But it was more than that. The Colonial identity drew heavily on the literary tradition of writers such as Rider Haggard, John Buchan, and Rudyard Kipling. Theirs was a tradition of adventurousness and self-sufficiency, a tradition drawn from living abroad, far from the "mother country", amid exotic peoples and challenging physical conditions. Often, colonial children, like myself and my father, were sent away for schooling, typically to England, as early as 6 or 7 years of age. Boarding school, and the baggage it carried, played an important part in forming our characters. Reactions were varied. Some dug in to their old traditions, to the world in which they were comfortable. They became more British than the British. They drank in the all-English bars, played cricket, sailed, and seldom conversed with the local population except in the roles of master and servant. These tended to become racist and insular, yearning for an imperial Britain whose sun had already set. Others reveled in the polyglot, multi-cultural nature of their lives, and absorbed all that they found around them. Our childhood drew on all these elements.

As I entered my teenage years, my mind was still a sponge. While the world described by Kipling and Rider Haggard and John Buchan filled my early imagination, others more concrete inspired me too. My father had a book on great explorers, whose exploits were yet more tangible than those of the literary heroes. Men like:

James Cook, who sailed around the world and explored the Pacific Islands in the 1770s.

Ernest Shackleton, who failed to reach the South Pole, but documented extraordinary tales of courage and endurance while he and his men – all of whom survived – passed two winters stranded on the Antarctic ice. His classic advertisement for team members read: *"Wanted. Men for hazardous journey. Low wages. Bitter cold. Long hours of complete darkness. Safe return doubtful. Honour and recognition in the event of success."*

Robert Scott and Lawrence Oates, who both died after reaching the South Pole thirty-six days after the Norwegian Roald Amundsen. Oates, who was suffering from frostbite, walked out of his tent during a blizzard, and died, in order to give his comrades an increased chance of surviving. His parting words were: *"I am just going outside, and may be some time."*

David Livingstone, who explored the Zambezi and was the first European to see the Victoria Falls.

John Hanning Speke, who discovered the source of the Nile flowing from the northern tip of Lake Victoria.

and above all

Sir Richard Burton[3]. One of my childhood heroes. The stuff of myths and legends. A character so bold, and inquisitive, adventurous and brave, that he could not fail to ignite the heart of one as impressionable as I. Burton was born at the beginning of the great Victorian age (1821 to be precise) in England. He spoke over 20 languages fluently, and not just the standard European languages. He was also proficient in Arabic and in several Indian and African languages. He studied and was accepted as a master by the gurus of a Tantric Hindu sect, and by the Qadiri brotherhood of Sufism. He explored great swaths of East Africa and was one of the first Europeans to visit Mecca, a journey of great peril.

Burton personifies one element of the British Empire that we lack today. There was a sense among the British Empire builders that nothing was impossible. No place too far or too perilous to reach. No aspect of scientific knowledge too complex to study. No country so barbaric that it could not be tamed and civilized by the hand of colonial rule. Call it arrogance. Call it hubris. And it was both of these. But, in its best incarnation, the Empire provided the channel for the energies and desires of a creative, adventurous, formidable people. A channel for them to undertake journeys of internal and external discovery and accomplishment that are hard to find today. While this sense is now rare among Britons at home or abroad, it was very much a part of the white settler spirit, and part of our lives in East Africa. The commitment to seek and confront challenge was conscious in the men and women of my father's generation, and it was certainly an unconscious part of the identity of the youth of my generation. In the Colonial spirit, intellectual exploration is placed on an even footing with the risk of danger, the chance to fail and the opportunity to respond to the danger in a manner that forces young people to discover their inner initiative, their inner strength.

It was my good fortune that my parents subscribed to this view of personal development. Many are my memories of activities that challenged us and, when accomplished, gave us an enormous sense of independence and power that no amount of cossetting, encouragement or parental praise could provide. The ring of islands around Dar es Salaam, and the wondrous, breeze-rich, Indian Ocean, were one source of such challenge …. and the cause of my mother's anguish. At 16, I was an avid sailor. My father owned a 505, a racing machine designed for two adults, one of whom is attached to a "trapeze", a cable from ¾ way up the mast from which the crew hangs out with the soles of his feet planted on the side of the boat. I had figured out that if I created a very long extension to the tiller, I could sail the 505 by myself, attached to the trapeze and helming at the same time. And, on many a weekday, I would do precisely that, sailing out to the islands by myself, enjoying immensely both the sense of independent accomplishment that came from being on my own on that ocean and the wonder of being at one with Nature, not to mention the occasional buzz of adrenalin that would come as the breeze picked up and the 505 began to skid across the waves like the racing machine it was designed to be.

Some years ago I asked my aging mother how she felt about her son venturing out on these myriad adventures. She told me she was terrified, and recounted the following story.

Unbeknownst to me, my mother one day spotted me a kilometer or so out to sea, alone on the 505. She parked, with anxious, fearful heart, on a point near the mouth of the harbor, to watch and ensure I came to no harm. After I sailed back closer to shore she drove away, relieved, and did not say anything to me. But she did confront my father, asking him to place limits on my adventurousness. His reply, according to my mother was simply: "Leave the boy alone. He will be fine. Anyway," he said, "Better drowned than Duffer." A Duffer is an old English nautical term for a sailor who has not learned the ropes and is likely to be at risk, or worse, to be a hazard to others, in the event of a storm at sea. My mother never told me how she reacted to this view of child raising, but suffice to say, no word was ever mentioned about my solo trips on the 505 and the trapeze.

Although born in Kenya, I did not have the sense of being Kenyan that I later acquired. But nor did I feel Tanzanian. Unlike Kenya, the European population of Tanzania was too small, and too transient, to have its own identity. In 1931 the European population of Tanganyika was 7,500. In 1963, a generation later, the total European population had grown by less than 4,000 and was under 12,000. The African population, on the other hand, had grown by almost 5 million, and was in excess of 9.5 million. With the exception of some German families who had moved to Tanganyika before the First World War and had started farms on the foothills of Kilimanjaro and in the Usambara Mountains, the number of Europeans who had lived in Tanganyika for more than a generation, was probably less than 1,000. We did not have the vested interest in Tanganyika that the white settlers of Kenya or Rhodesia had in their countries. We did not identify with Tanganyika as our country. Nor did most of us identify with any other country in particular. Our family had been away from our roots for three generations, on both sides of the family. On the surface we were simply British Colonial kids, but it was more complex because our parents fell outside the stereotype. There was a European varnish thinly glossed on top of the British Colonial spirit of inquisitiveness, adventure and "better drowned than duffer". If asked, Alan would have identified himself as Irish, and Jeannine would have identified herself as French. I think they felt more European than British. Caitlín was sent to school in France at 9 years old. I was permitted to travel alone to France at 14, and we both studied in Italy after High School and before University. When we knelt by the bedside in the evenings ("the family that prays together stays together"), Alan would end the prayers with a short litany of prayers for divine assistance in a variety of European languages: *Santa Maria de los Angeles, Resa por Nosotros. Sante Jeanne d'Arc, La Pucelle d'Orleans, Priez pour Nous. Santo Francesco de Assisi, Prega per noi.*

CHAPTER 7

MASSACRE AND REVOLUTION

1959 – 1964

In 1959, Dingle Foot was the Labour MP for Ipswich, in Suffolk. He had been a prominent barrister and had defended several high profile Kenyans during the early 1950's, including Chief Koinange, one of the leaders of the KAU. During this period, Foot and Barclay became good friends, and when Barclay retired and Foot became a Member of Parliament, they often dined together in my grandparents' apartment, walking distance from the Houses of Parliament. One evening in June, Foot came over to the apartment to seek Barclay's advice. "The information that I am about to share with you," he told Barclay, "is confidential, and not in the public domain. But Members of Parliament have the information and there is to be a closed door debate at the end of this month." This information, it transpired, was not only more instrumental in the acceleration of the dismantling of the British Empire than all the rebellions and fires set by the local populations, but it also led to my sister and me being sent to school in England and France, respectively, that autumn. The account that follows is taken in large part from the records of the parliamentary debates, and other documents released in 2009, fifty years after the incident described by Foot. Obviously, neither I nor my father was present at the conversation between Foot and Barclay, but Barclay spoke to Alan about it and strongly recommended that Caitlín and I leave Tanganyika for a while.

THE HOLA MASSACRE IN 1959

Kenya had instituted the Emergency Regulations in 1952, and these remained in place until the end of the decade. One of the features of the Emergency was the Government's power to arrest and detain suspected Mau Mau sympathisers without trial. In 1959, long after the Mau Mau threat had subsided, some 85 of these detainees were being held in a camp in the Northeastern desert between the coast and Mount Kenya, near the village of Hola. This land is an arid, semi-desert, scrubland. It is hot and inhospitable. It could not be further, neither geographically, not climactically, from the wet, wooded, mountains of central Kenya that the Kikuyu called home. The camp was squalid, with miserable conditions, and sparse rations. Most of the detainees had been detained without trial. They were political prisoners, held on suspicion of having affiliations with the Mau Mau. It was the view of John Cowan, the Superintendent of Prisons that the "rehabilitation" of these "prisoners" would be accelerated if they were made to work, and that if they refused to do so they should be "manhandled" and "forced to carry out the task." And so he ordered.

On the morning of March 3, the eighty five detainees at the Hola camp were marched to a barren stretch of land and directed to dig an irrigation ditch, using their bare hands and small primitive tools, since picks and shovels in the hands of prisoners were considered too dangerous. The detainees refused, and stayed seated in a tight group in a *wadi* some twelve feet deep. Enraged by the obstinacy of the prisoners, the Camp

Superintendent, Mr. Sullivan, then blew his whistle, upon which command the *askaris* drew their truncheons and other sticks, and began to beat the detainees as they crouched together on the ground. James Muigai, one of the survivors, testified that he remembered the order being issued in Swahili: *Piga mpaka wafanye kazi* (Flog them until they work). The beating lasted nigh on three hours. At this point, exhausted, the *askaris* withdrew. Eleven men lay dead; almost all the others had suffered serious wounds. Fractured ribs, cracked skulls, and heavy bruises over large parts of their bodies.

The British authorities tried to cover up or gloss over the incident. Men died from "drinking poisoned water" read the first reports. Prison Officer Walter Coutts told the inquest that the men "willed themselves to death". The Attorney General of Kenya, Eric Griffith Jones, claimed that there was insufficient evidence to prosecute because the identity of the *askaris* who rained the blows on the prisoners was not known (although, of course, the identity of the white wardens who ordered the beatings was very well known). The matter was, as one low level Kenyan official put it *"best dealt with quietly"*.

The Parliamentary reports of debates on July 27, 1959, show a House divided. Some members preferred to overlook the facts, referring to the prisoners as "sub-human creatures".[k] Others were outraged and incensed. Dingle Foot was among those who spoke most forcefully against the actions of the Kenya Government. He accused the Government of using the Emergency Powers in a way that was wholly unconstitutional, counter-productive, and certain

---

k Hansard: HC Deb 27 July 1959, vol 610 cc 181-262.

to cause more harm than good. He gave the following account of how perverted the system had become:

"Let me tell the House of an experience of mine when I was in Kenya four years ago. I went to visit the detainees on Manda Island. At that time it was almost an article of faith among many people in Kenya that those on Manda Island were the blackest of the Mau Mau offenders, but when I went there, and when I saw the grounds for detention which had been supplied to the detainees when they went before the Advisory Committee, I found in some cases which I saw that it was not even suggested that they had taken a Mau Mau oath or that they had engaged in any form of Mau Mau activity whatsoever. They were in prison because they had made inflammatory speeches or because they associated with somebody else who had been sent to prison or, in one case, as was said of one man, "You were the editor of a near-seditious newspaper which has since been suppressed."

One sees how this process goes on. First, they take emergency powers. Then they suppress the newspaper. What a "near-seditious" newspaper is I do not know, but they suppress a newspaper and call it near-seditious, and then they say to the man, "Because you were the editor of the suppressed newspaper, therefore we are going to lock you up not for a short time but for a period of many years." Many of those on Manda Island referred to as Mau Mau detainees were in fact nothing more than political prisoners."

Enoch Powell, a young conservative backbencher who would later emerge as a leader of the right wing of his party, argued forcefully;

All Government, all influence of man upon man, rests upon opinion. What we can do in Africa, where we still govern, and where we no longer govern, depends upon the opinion which is entertained of the way in which this country acts and the way in which Englishmen act. We cannot, we dare not, in Africa of all places, fall below our own highest standards in the acceptance of responsibility."

At the highest levels of the British Government this massacre ignited a realization that the time for British withdrawal from Africa had come. In January, 1960, in a speech in Accra, Ghana, Harold Macmillan, then Prime Minister, announced:

The wind of change is blowing through this continent. Whether we like it or not, this growth of national consciousness is a political fact. We must all accept it as a fact, and our national policies must take account of it.

With this wind of change came a rapid divestment of Britain's African colonies[4]. Nigeria in 1960, Tanganyika and Sierra Leone in 1961, Uganda in 1962, Kenya in 1963, Malawi and Zambia in 1964. Not all went according to plan. South Africa declared itself a Republic in 1961, and Rhodesia issued its Unilateral Declaration of Independence in 1965. Settler reaction in Kenya and Rhodesia was essentially tribal. The settlers dug in with a sense of embattled determination. It was their (white) tribe against the rest. They felt they had brought "civilization" to the Dark Continent, they had developed the land, brought in cash crops, built roads and railways.

They felt they had as much right as any other person, white or black, to their land, their privileges and their patronage. They feared expulsion, bloodshed, the loss of their lands, an uncertain future.

For white Colonials, the 1960's were an unsettled and unsettling time. It was the decade in which thirty-two countries in Africa attained their independence, seventeen of them in 1960. Although the hand-over from the British authorities to the new African governments was generally peaceful[5] (Rhodesia being the glaring exception), the French and Belgian experience was disastrous.[6] But change in a continent, in a country, in a society, takes many forms and wears many faces. Like a teenage child coming of age, Africa wore one face for the public, another face for its friends, and harbored still another face within. At the most visible level there was the pomp and circumstance of the handing over of power, followed either by peaceful transition, or by bloodshed, genocide and the settling of old grudges. At another level, at the level of the lives of every day people, so long as blood was not running in the streets, the change was gradual. The Europeans retired to their privileged residential areas, but remained unmolested by the change in government. In Tanzania, we continued to sail on Sundays, play golf on Wednesdays, and drink sundowners with friends on the balconies of the houses overlooking the sea. The Indian population kept the wheels of commerce turning, and the vast majority of the African population knew no change. At a third level, the intrigues of West vs. East, the tug of war between the capitalist/imperial presence vs. the subtle insinuation of Chinese influence, played an important role. These changes were not always apparent, but they crept upon us, creating unease and fear.

Beyond its borders, on all sides, Tanganyika witnessed change. But, at least for a while, Tanganyika was an island in a blood-torn continent, and Dar es Salaam was indeed a Haven of Peace. There was none of the tension that dominated our neighbours. The European population was small, concentrated in Dar es Salaam, and had very little social interaction with the local Africans. We knew the "houseboys" who cooked and cleaned, the *syces* who groomed and exercised the horses, and the *msafiri* who polished the winches on the sailboats, sanded and varnished their hulls, and had them rigged and ready to go when we arrived. But our interaction was minimal. My father knew the new President, Julius Nyerere,[7] the leader of the Tanganyika African National Union Party ("TANU"), and indeed he paid several social visits to our home in the months prior to Independence. Nyerere wanted to start a relationship, an informal one-on-one relationship, with Alan, who ran the Tanganyika Standard and controlled the voice of the major source of news.

In the years immediately following Tanganyika's independence, however, the tiny white population in Tanganyika, looked in horror across our borders at the brutality of white rulers on black ruled, at the irresponsible and hasty departure of France and Belgium leaving many of their colonies in the hands of uneducated thugs and military men, and above all, at the civil wars that were beginning to burst like random fireworks round Africa. In March 1960, sixty-nine Africans were killed in the infamous Sharpeville massacre in South Africa. On Tanganyika's western border, the civil war raged in the Congo. On its southern border, the Mozambique Liberation Front (Frelimo) was mounting violent attacks on the Portuguese rulers. Frelimo set up its headquarters in Dar es Salaam. Tanganyika was surrounded by, and was being dragged into, the wars for freedom from white rule.

Then, in January 1964, the violence hit home.

Early on the morning of Sunday, January 12, 1964, Alan was loading the car to go to the Yacht Club. Swimsuits, goggling equipment, spear gun, flippers, a new block to fit at the foot of the mast. Jeannine was wrapping and packing the picnic lunch that they would enjoy with their friends Joy and John Bellamy. They planned to sail out to Bongoyo Island, swim and goggle a little, and then enjoy lunch with a couple of Tusker beers. The phone rang. Jeannine answered.

"Hello".

"May I speak to Mr. Alan Nihill?" An African voice. Unfamiliar. With less accent than a houseboy or one of the servants.

"Who is calling?"

"I am calling from the office of the President."

"What President?" Jeannine asked, confused.

"President Julius Nyerere, madam."

Now she was really confused; confused and flustered. "Is this a hoax" she thought, but decided it was not.

"Oh, OK. Hold on a minute. I'll see if I can get him."

Running out to the garage, Jeannine blurted:

"It's the President. President Nyerere. Wants to talk to you. On the phone."

Alan looked at her puzzled, as though she was talking nonsense.

"Hurry. He's waiting."

Dropping the flippers and spear gun on the garage floor, Alan leapt to the phone. "What on earth could this be about?" he thought. There had not been any stories recently that could have caused problems with the government. On the couple of occasions when he had been summoned to Government House, it had been to discuss stories that were perceived to be dangerous to the Government. Although the Press was still free to write what it wished, Alan understood that the Tanganyika Standard was the most widely read newspaper, a reference watched and picked up by other newspapers abroad, and he shared with the President the sense that the newspaper had an obligation to consider the interests of the Republic when publishing stories. The era of yellow journalism, and investigative reporting had not yet arrived in Africa.

As he was ushered into the Presidential Office, Alan noted the large number of Government servants milling around. "Strange for a Sunday", he thought. The offices were simple. Left over from colonial times. Signs of decay. Peeling paint, dark smudges where old photographs had been removed, electrical fittings that had been haphazardly torn out and not replaced, lanterns without light bulbs.

"Good morning, Alan. How good of you to come on such short notice." The President greeted him warmly. Although they had only met a few times since the first visit to our home in August 1960, they had a respectful personal relationship.

"Of course, Mr. President. It is my honor to be here."

"Sit down. Sit down, please." Nyerere motioned to Alan to sit in the armchair to his left, and then, turning to the assistant: "*Unaweza kwenda, sasa.*" You may go now.

"Alan, have you heard about what is going on in Zanzibar?" the President asked.

"No, Sir, I have not."

"Well, last night a group of men led by a Mr. Okelo, took over, as they say, "the reins of power". To be more precise, shortly after midnight, one of the senior men in Government was woken up with a pistol to his stomach and a bow and arrow to his throat, and told to accompany the assailant to the Radio Station where he was directed to instruct the assailant and his men in how to use the radio. Shortly afterwards, Mr. Okelo personally overcame a guard in the Sultan's Palace and, with a small handful of men, took over control of the place. Many of the Sultan's family were rounded up, but the Sultan, apparently, escaped. Mr. Okelo is transmitting on the radio, announcing the overthrow of the government, which, as you know is dominated by men of Arab descent, loyal to the Sultan. Unfortunately his message is far from peaceful. Indeed it is full of emotional language of hatred toward the Arab rulers. This is very disconcerting to us. Now, I have called you in here because you need to know what is going on, and to help us ensure matters don't get out of control."

"Yes, Sir. I understand. May I ask, Who is this fellow, Okelo. I have not heard of him before. I thought the opposition was led by men like Karume and Sheik Baba. What is their reaction?"

"Okelo is a thug. He is not part of the political process, and he does not have our support. We need to deal carefully with him. He acted on his own, much to our annoyance. As you can imagine, the members of the Afro Shirazi Party, led by Karume, had plans of their own for the overthrow of the Arab regime. We did not object to their plans, although I did speak to Amani [Karume] and stressed the need for any overthrow to be peaceful and without bloodshed."

"Do you know Okelo?"

"No. But what we are hearing is very disturbing. They say he is not even from here, he is Ugandan. We are receiving reports that armed bands, of African people, are rounding up people of Arab descent and corralling them into compounds. The situation is very delicate, and if Okelo is left to stir up hatred the way he is doing, we could have extensive bloodshed. There is a lot of pent up hatred against the Arabs for the way they have ruled the island for generations. I want you to know that we are NOT in favor of this behavior, and we will do what we can behind the scenes to minimize the violence. Both Karume and Baba are in Dar es Salaam today, but they should be boarding ship today and heading back to Zanzibar as soon as possible."

"So, with respect to the Standard, Sir. What is it that you are thinking?"

"Alan, you know as well as I do that our young African democracies are fragile. The Congo became a blood bath within months of Independence. On our southern border there is war in Mozambique, and Rhodesia is not far from being in the same state. Newly independent Kenya, to our north, is in an uneasy balance. And now, not fifty miles off our shores, Zanzibar, which gained its independence only months ago, could also become a blood bath. We must avoid any sensational reporting, stories that could make the international community, or even the European and Indian communities within our country, think that Tanganyika is at risk of falling into the same chaos. We are not at risk, and I will see to it that such chaos does not occur here. We are a peaceful country, and we will ensure that the violence in Zanzibar does not spill over to here. Do you understand?"

Alan left Government House quite shaken. The interview had lasted less than half an hour, but it was clear to him that the rebellion in Zanzibar was dangerous not just for the Arab leaders of Zanzibar, but for the peace and stability of Tanganyika, and indeed of Eastern

Africa. He called home to say that he would not be sailing with Jeannine and their friends, that she should not worry, but that he would talk with her that evening. "Oh, and don't say anything to Joy or John about the call. Just tell them that something came up at work and that I will try to catch up with you and them at the club for a sundowner."

Jeannine struggled all day to retain a calm composure, but her sixth sense, that fey intuition of hers, was vibrating. By the time she got home, and was able to sit down with Alan, she was a bundle of nerves.

"So, what did the President want?" she asked, bluntly. Alan was evasive. Where is the line between what you can discuss with your wife, and things that are matters of State, to be kept inside? How do Prime Ministers and Presidents the world over create Chinese walls between their personal and private lives?

"Some trouble in Zanzibar, it seems. We need to keep on top of it, be sure we know what is really going on. Front page tomorrow."

"Some Bloody trouble, is it. What does that mean? We live here, and our children live here, and we are trying to make a life for them. I can tell you what bloody trouble. Everyone at the bar at the Club can tell you what Bloody trouble. The Africans have staged a revolution and are out in the streets killing all the Arabs. They say it's a massacre. Not just Arabs, but anyone who is Muslim. It's the Congo. It's Algeria. It's Mau Mau all over again. I thought we had left all that behind, and here we are again, with Africans killing Europeans and Arabs."

Jeannine broke down, sobbing convulsively, distraught.

"Now, now darling. No need to get hysterical. No Europeans have been killed. In fact, I understand that the Europeans are being treated very well. This is not about us."

"What do you mean "not about us"?" she cried. "Of course it's about us. It's about whoever is in power in Africa, and the Africans turning them out. It's the Communists. Did you know that Sheik Baba has been obtaining weapons from the communists? Did you know we are going to have a bunch of bloody Chinese and Russians on our doorstep? Its worse than Cuba."

The argument lasted well into the night. Jeannine crying, pleading with Alan for the family to leave. She did not know where to. Maybe to France, or to Ireland. Anywhere but more of Africa. Alan calming her, reminding her of all the wonderful things we shared and experienced; explaining how Zanzibar was different, how Tanganyika was different.

A week later, the army, the Tanganyika African Rifles, still under the command of British officers, revolted, and the British officers were evacuated to Kenya. Troops roamed the streets of Dar es Salaam, in open jeeps, machine guns in their hands. Shops were looted and the air was redolent with the scent of an impending Congo-like disaster. Jeannine, and many other women and children, sought refuge in the High Commissioner's home.

In the end Alan was right. The army revolt was put down within a week, primarily because Nyerere called in British troops from the nearby warship *Centaur*, to intervene. In Zanzibar, although there was widespread killing of Arabs in the days immediately following the revolution, Nyerere quickly and carefully orchestrated a merger of the two countries, resulting in what is now Tanzania. Karume was appointed Vice President. Okelo was denied entry after a trip outside the country, and Sheik Baba was arrested and tried for an alleged plot to overthrow the Government. Peace returned to Tanzania. But Jeannine's fears were not unfounded, and Africa was no long safe for white colonials.

CHAPTER 8

ROMAN CATHOLICS, RUSSIAN

ORTHODOX, AND HUMANISTS

Although the details of Hola were not made public until fifty years later, Barclay knew them, and discussed the situation with Alan. In the autumn of 1960, months after the Hola hearings in Parliament, and shortly before Tanganyikan independence, I was pulled from Soni and sent to Gilling Castle, the preparatory school for Ampleforth College in the North Yorkshire moors.

Alan's contract with the Tanganyika Standard provided for one free airfare Dar/London/Dar each year for each child, and one round trip for him and Jeannine every two years. So, August 1960, a DC 10, (the kind of plane that took Ingrid Bergman out of Casablanca, as Humphrey Bogart wished her well: "Here's Looking at You Kid") is revving up its twin props as I enter the awkwardly cantilevered fuselage. I am not alone, or friendless. They called it the Lollipop Special, a charter flight for Tanganyika's colonial schoolchildren off to boarding school and another six or nine months away from their families. Two days flying. One night in a sweltering, miserable airport hotel because the DC 10 does not have night flight capability. Dar to Tanga; Tanga to Arusha; Arusha to Nairobi; Nairobi to Kampala; Kampala to Khartoum; Khartoum to Wadi Halfa. Night in Wadi Halfa, steamy hot, Sahara desert without air conditioning, the Sudan side of the great Aswan dam on the border with Egypt. The day breaks and we are off to Cairo; Cairo to Tunis; Tunis to Malta; Malta to Rome; Rome to Paris; and on to London. Up down, up down, take off and landing; air sick bags on the ready for each descent. It's miserable. In later years I was introduced to the 30,000 club. Never a member, always an outsider, yearning to be part of this elite group. The Greek and Italian boys somehow seemed to comprise most of the membership. One wonders whether it was really because they had girlfriends who were eager to join them in the cramped quarters of the bathroom while the plane was at altitude, or because we never questioned the veracity of their claims.

While not actually in school, I stayed with my grandparents, Nuala and Barclay. They lived in the top floor apartment by Westminster Cathedral, the Catholic Cathedral, not to be confused with Westminster Abbey, although they are less than a mile apart. While it was a relatively chic area of London, I suspect that the reason they lived there is because Nuala was a devout Catholic and would go to Mass every morning. She loved the Latin liturgy and was "at sea" when Vatican II, initiated by the great John Paul XXIII, instituted Mass in the vernacular. Only a handful of churches in the mid '60s offered Mass in Latin, and Nuala would travel to Farm Street, in Mayfair, to hear Mass in the traditional Latin liturgy which she knew by heart. We would kneel in the living room every evening, reciting the rosary. All five decades of the Rosary, ten Hail Marys, an Our Father, and a Glory Be in each decade. These Rosary sessions were attacked with the energy of a racehorse at the gates of the Grand National or the Kentucky Derby. Barclay and I would start:

Hail Mary fullofgrace
The Lord is with thee
Blessed art thouamongwomen
And Blessed is the fruit of thywombJesus

Before the 4th line had started, Nuala was off to the races, intoning her segment, the second half of the prayer:

Holy Mary, Mother of God
Pray for us sinners
Now, and at the hourofourdeath
Amen

We recited this mantra ten times, and then the break for the Our Father and the Glory Be, before setting off at another galloping decade of Hail Mary's.

Barclay's Catholicism was as strong, maybe stronger, but less devout. He came to the Church voluntarily, intellectually accepting, as a History Major at Cambridge, that the actions of Henry VIII, his desire for a son thwarted by a series of barren wives, were not justification enough to cause the establishment of a new Religion. But Nuala knew, and enforced, the rules, the little rules that define a religion when it loses its touch with spirituality.

7.20 a.m. Sunday. Breakfast is over and we are cleaning the table. Nuala is washing up. Mass will be at 10.00 and Communion will be at 10.30. The rules require three hours of abstinence before partaking in Communion. As we are picking up, Barclay teaches me a game.

"Place a peanut in the palm of your left hand." He does so, adjusting his feet so that they are stable, sturdy and some two feet apart.

"Keep the hand stiff. Don't bend it. Then, positioning your hand carefully below your mouth, thus" and he positions his hand about waist level, "form a fist with your right hand and thump your left hand just where the thumb meets the wrist." Whack. The peanut bounces up like a bullet, straight into his waiting, open mouth.

"You try it."

OK, I position myself, peanut in the palm of the hand, and Whack, but the peanut bounces flaccidly to the floor.

"You tried to anticipate and to propel the peanut with your left hand. No need to do that. When you whack your left hand with your right the reaction is instinctive and the peanut will shoot right up. Try again. No, no, not so close to the mouth. Lower the hand to waist level."

After a few tries, the knack is coming to me, the peanuts are hitting their mark until Nuala arrives at the dining room door wondering what happened to the dirty dishes.

"What on earth are you two thinking? It's now 7.30 and Communion will be in less than three hours. Do you realize that because of your silly game, and eating the peanuts, you will not be able to participate in Communion."

I slump down into the chair and rock backwards.

"Don't rock the chair, you barbaric child. Those are two hundred year old Chippendale."

I must have had that phrase hurled at me fifty times before I learned to sit still and not rock. I believe it honestly hurt her to see her grandchildren growing up with such rotten manners: failing to stand up when a lady entered the room, eating with one's mouth "full" (even though it may be but a morsel), placing one's hands above the table rather than below (in contrast to the French etiquette which preferred the hands in a light fist resting on the table), and of course, worst of all, not following the maxim that "Little children should be seen and not heard." Neither Caitlín nor I was much good at being seen and not heard. If the conversation was interesting, we wanted our voice to be heard.

Much of our poor education Nuala laid, unfairly, at Jeannine's doorstep: "The French don't understand good manners. Its no wonder you never learn." Occasionally she would comment, not in reference to her daughter in law, but generally, "Africa begins at Calais", which is really quite unfair since she had a great respect for the Chinese and the Persian empires. Despite her Irish upbringing and the sense of independent Irish identity evidenced by her father, Joseph O'Carroll – who rejected a knighthood offered by Queen Victoria, announcing: "She is not My Queen," – Nuala liked being Lady Nihill. She read the Telegraph Obituaries and Weddings columns every day, commenting on the deceased and the betrothed that she knew. When Barclay had to go to hospital for an operation in the mid '60s, she took me aside to tell me about the condition. "He has prostate cancer," she said, not explaining what the prostate was or why it needed an operation. "This is a perfectly acceptable illness. Indeed, Harold Macmillan, the former Prime Minister, had it." As though there were some illnesses that attacked respectable folks, and others that only attacked the working poor. It did not occur to her to let me know whether it was serious or not, whether he was in pain etc. She was comforted by the fact that Macmillan had had the same condition.

Trivial, frivolous pursuits were not condoned. On Saturdays Barclay and I enjoyed watching the races on television. The Friday edition of the Evening News listed all the races, the horses, the races they had run and how they had placed, the jockey, his weight and recent results, the handicaps, in short everything you needed to make a measured judgment and place a bet. But Barclay was forbidden to bet. I suspect that he had lost some money, or else it was just Nuala's way of indicating that she did not approve of this pastime.

"Just popping out to the corner to buy some cigarettes," he would say as we squirreled out of the apartment to place a bet.

"Don't you be going by those bookies again and wasting your money on foolish bets."

"Back in a minute" he would reply without acknowledging her comment. Nuala would often tell me:

"His deafness is getting worse all the time. Terrible affliction for me, you know."

But it was my sense that Barclay was mostly deaf when in her company. Certainly, at the bookies or at the Fulham Football Club grounds, he was not deaf, and enjoyed a good chat with the local lads.

Although the world of grandparents-in-London was the opposite of the life-by-the ocean Dar es Salaam, and much less fun, it had its advantages, and Nuala was an important part of that. Her discipline and rigor were a great counterweight for a child raised with few boundaries. In Dar es Salaam my mind grew through exploration, through touch and feel and physical experience. In London she trained it to grow through reading, through thinking, through abstract experience. She found a book called I Spy London, and we would explore the city, by bus, finding old tombs, statues of poets, homes of artists, and a myriad other esoteric shadows of London past. The Tate Gallery, Covent Garden, Kensington Gardens, rowing down the Thames, she introduced me to them all, with a teaching style that was not didactic but fascinated. Fascinated and consequently fascinating. Madame Tussauds for a bit of history. Hyde Park to listen to the speakers, many of them Kenyan in those days, ranting against British rule. And music. One afternoon I was in my room in their apartment listening to music. I had developed a taste for Piaf, and happened to be listening to *La vie en Rose,* when Nuala entered. She didn't say a word. Just started humming and then dancing, small steps first, then more pronounced. Almost in a trance, as though I were not there. What memory chords was this music strumming? What distant lover was present in the room? I never asked.

Like Soni, Ampleforth too was an all-boys' Catholic boarding school, but run by Benedictine monks, rather than Rosminian priests. I don't know what it is about monks, but the ones I knew at Ampleforth were wonderfully gentle, caring, spiritual people. Maybe it is their commitment to prayer and contemplation, rather than to action (unlike many priests, and especially priests who are sent to distant lands to serve). Maybe, in the case of the monks of Ampleforth, it was the high level of education they had received. Maybe it was their liberal understanding of free will, choice, and the rights of Man. Maybe it was the school's commitment to service to others less privileged. One of the monks who most impacted me was Father Basil Hume. At the time, he was the Abbot of the Monastery. He went on to become Archbishop of Westminster and then Cardinal. He was bright (Oxford trained), athletic (an excellent rugby player), what used to be known as a "muscular Catholic". His commitment to service was palpable, and in his sermons, which typically were very short, 4 or 5 minutes at most, he ingrained in us that although we were a privileged group of boys and young men, this privilege came from God, and with this privilege came the responsibility to serve.

Whatever it was, the experience was totally different from that of Soni. Ampleforth was one of those extraordinary schools where no one was a star, no one was special, everyone had to participate in every activity (including boxing, music, cross country running, and woodwork), but somehow students were able to find their special talent and excel. In my year were: Anthony Gormley, probably the most famous English sculptor alive today; Julian Fellowes, author and Director of Downton Abbey; and, a few years older, Tony Bucknall, captain of the English Rugby team.

In April 1966, coincident with my 16th birthday, a group of us from Ampleforth had the enormous good fortune to visit Russia. One of the monks, Father Francis, spoke Russian and was involved with the Russian exile community in London. He worked periodically with the BBC on Russian history and art programs, and was close to many in the BBC hierarchy. Father Francis arranged for a group of Ampleforth boys to be invited to Russia, with sponsorship of the BBC who would prepare a documentary about aspects of the trip. The timing was extraordinary. Internally, Russia was sliding back to the repression of the Stalin era. Yuli Daniel and Andrei Sinyavsky, both prominent writers, were put on trial—the first such public trials since Stalin's day. The powers and the reach of the KGB were expanded under the new premier, Leonid Brezhnev. The Vietnam War had escalated dramatically with the arrival of U.S.

ground troops in 1965, and Russian/US/European relations were at a low. Few westerners visited Russia. The invitation to a group of English schoolboys, Catholic schoolboys from a monastery school no less, was a trial balloon.

The highlight of the trip, and clearly the reason why Ampleforth was interested in supporting the trip, was a visit to the Lavra Monastery in Zagorsk, some 70 kilometers north east of Moscow. Founded in 1345, Lavra was, until the Russian Revolution, the center of the Russian Orthodox Church. It housed a unique collection of manuscripts, religious icons, paintings, and other artifacts. In 1917, it was closed and not re-opened as a church until the 1940s when Stalin began to permit some minimal religious activity in Russia. In 1966, it was still one of the very few places in Russia where Russian Orthodox priests and monks could worship openly. The goal for Ampleforth was for its boys to participate in the ceremony of Easter Sunday midnight Mass, a breakthrough in relations between the Orthodox Church and the Catholic Church, but also a courageous step in the opening of Russia to the West. In some ways it was similar to Nixon's Ping-Pong diplomacy with China five years later.

As we rode the train across northern Europe, through East Germany (the Berlin Wall had been erected five years earlier), through Poland and into Russia, we learned and practiced singing the Kyrie Eleison, the Gloria, and the Sanctus, all intrinsic parts of the Mass celebration, in Russian.

Within the Lavra Monastery is a cathedral, the Cathedral of the Assumption. The Easter vigil service had started earlier, but we arrived shortly before midnight. There was no electricity, no doubt a concession to religion that the Communist State considered going too far. So the cathedral was lit by thousands of candles and lanterns. The elaborate chandeliers twinkled with a hundred candles on each. The pillars held oil lanterns burning openly. And every person in the vast expanse of the cathedral carried a candle. The orthodox priests all seemed to be six feet tall, with long, flowing black beards, and black cassocks. Their presence was overwhelming, their deep, bass and baritone voices thunderously proclaiming the Mass and chanting the liturgy. All around was the smell and smoke of incense emanating from ornate gold thuribles decorated with twelve little bells representing the twelve apostles.

As the moment came for the singing of the Kyrie Eleison, twenty six fresh-faced, cleanly dressed, nervous boys stepped onto the altar and responded, some still with treble voices, to the opening bars sung by the Patriarch himself. The cathedral was packed, wall-to-wall, tight with people holding candles, standing with barely enough room to shift their feet. What I saw was a sea of faces. Not just any faces. They were the faces of women in their sixties and older, women who were Orthodox Christians before the Revolution and who had held on to the faith of their fathers and mothers in spite, as the hymn goes, "in spite of dungeon, fire and sword." Few were the faces of men, and even fewer the faces of young people. Dressed in black dresses, black scarfs covering their heads, with wrinkled, sun-dried skin, and the gnarled hands of peasants, these women began to cry. They cried at the hope that there would be another day for their faith, that young people would once again populate their churches and cathedrals, that their God was returning to them after fifty years of isolation. And through their tears there emerged an immensely powerful swell of sound, of chant, of joy, as they answered the refrain of the Kyrie Eleison, Christe Eleison, Kyrie Eleison.

This was an enormously moving emotional experience for all of us. But, my emotions were mixed. I saw and felt the depth of the faith of these women. I thought about those Catholic saints who held the flame through the years of Cromwell and beyond in England, who had died for their faith singing the praises of their Lord. This was the stuff of our Catholic education, and I had profound respect for what I saw. On the other hand, I asked myself how this God could leave these faithful women in the wilderness for fifty years. I thought of the Jews who fled from Egypt to Israel, but the thought gave me little comfort. I wondered at the elaborateness of the ceremony, the incense, the majestic singing, the size and presence of the priests, the ornateness of the cathedral, and compared it with simplicity of the Muslim mosques and prayer sessions. I reminisced about the playful friendliness of the Hindu Gods and asked myself why this Christian God was so distant and demanding. And finally, in a political moment, I reminisced on Mwalimu Nyerere's call for an egalitarian society, a society in which everyone was given the chance to start on an equal footing, with equal opportunity, and I measured that against the history of the Catholic and Anglican churches with which I was familiar, and found the latter to be lacking.

This was not the first time, nor would it be the last, that I felt myself standing apart from those with whom I lived, almost a spectator, fitting in to some extent, but still different. In Dar es Salaam we were outsiders, enjoying the ocean, the trout streams, the game parks, but always a race apart from almost everyone we saw in the streets, in the countryside. In England, I was with my age group,

I had friends, but they did not know Africa. They had not fallen asleep with the sound of lion roaring in the distance. They could not understand my relationship with the people and Nature. And now, again, I felt myself out of touch with my Catholic upbringing.

Goodall showed us how human animals can be. Ardrey and Morris showed us how our nature is derived from theirs. I wondered whether western philosophy would have been different if philosophers had known what we know today about our affinity with the animal world. Would their philosophizing have been different if, instead of starting from the premise, found in the Book of Genesis, that God made Man in His likeness, they had started from a completely different premise? Would the western mind have been conditioned to build its self-image upon the construct that our goal is to be closer to, and more like, a God who created us? Or would these philosophers have found a God in all that lives and breathes. A God, or pantheon, more akin to that of the Greeks, or of the Hindus. Gods who play a role in our lives and who struggle among themselves, who take sides and have favorites. Would they have entertained the possibility that we created God in our image and likeness, rather than the other way around? For me, Descartes' "I think therefore I am" did not go far enough. Do elephants "think"? Do hawks and bush babies? What does it mean, "to think"? Do sea slugs think? If not, do they exist?

I knew from my observations of animals, from the discoveries at Olduvai, and from the books that I read about the origins of Man, that I shared emotions with animals and that my ancestors had emerged from apes. I also knew, from my exposure to various religions that no religion holds a lock on the truth, and that the Gods of each reflect the culture of the followers. These thoughts and questions came to a head in religion class the following term. I announced to my religion teacher that I could not consider myself a Catholic, and that from now on I would be a Humanist. I did not know what that meant then, and I'm not sure I know now, but it felt good to affirm my independent thought and to base it on what I knew first hand.

Looking back, I was going through the classic conflict between the two great icons of European civilization: Socrates and Christ. Socrates, pillar of logic and realism. Christ, symbol of hope. Socrates, comfortable with the idea of death as an ultimate moment. Christ offering reasons to believe in a life after death. My African experience made me lean toward Socrates, at least at this stage in my life, and again in recent years. But, there were periods, most especially when we were raising children, that the clarity of values, the absence of relativism of the Church, the sense that we owed our children more reason to live than just that of a creature of the plains, caused me to re-evaluate that balance. As I grappled with the question of how should we raise our children, I read Francis Schaeffer's *How should we then live,* a brilliant apologia for Christianity, and William F. Buckley's *Nearer my God,* a riveting analysis of his faith, the questions, the enigmas, and, ultimately the leaps of faith that he made as a devout Catholic. In the end, we raised our children spiritually and socially Christian, but with little religious dogma or structure. Not a very effective balance.

DREAMING OF AMERICA

While the threat of war, the fear of instability, the image of blood in the streets, were the most obvious causes for concern, there were two other, more insidious factors at work, factors which ultimately disrupted our lives and caused us to move again. The first was the creeping influence of Russia, China and, above all, the ideology of Communism. The second was *Africanization.* But these pressures took time to develop. I jump ahead a decade. We still had several happy years left in the Haven of Peace.

The societal divisions within Tanganyika were imposed, largely, by economic and cultural forces. Race, per se, was not a dividing factor. Indeed, one of the charms of our life in Dar es Salaam, especially in the '60s after Tanganyika had gained independence, was the way in which we mixed freely with the Embassy crowd of all races, and with the emerging political class. No doubt our parents' open minds influenced this choice of friends. In my mid teens my friends included the two sons of the Somali ambassador, Ali and Mo (one wonders what kind of warlords they turned out to be); Ruby, the daughter of the Indonesian ambassador who captured my heart dancing the dance of the candles in the Balinese style, but whose rather intimidating older brother was always within sight; and Fatuma, an Egyptian girl whose parents were much more liberal than the current batch of Islamist Egyptians.

In the midst of this cultural melting pot, America held a special fascination for me. When President Kennedy inaugurated the U.S. AID (Agency for International Development) office in 1961, his words resonated across the third world:

"There is no escaping our obligations: our moral obligations as a wise leader and good neighbor in the interdependent community of free nations – our economic obligations as the wealthiest people in a world of largely poor people, as a nation no longer

dependent upon the loans from abroad that once helped us de-
velop our own economy – and our political obligations as the
single largest counter to the adversaries of freedom."

U.S. AID had a small office in the centre of town, and often, when my mother was shopping, she would drop me off there to browse the books and magazines in the library. There I found National Geographic, various newspapers, and big, glossy books with pictures of America. A country that welcomed the "poor and huddled masses", a country that dreamed of landing a man on the moon, a country whose President urged his fellow citizens to "ask not what your country can do for you; ask what you can do for your country", and who urged us, the citizens of the world to "ask what, together, we can do for the freedom of man." These words were writ large in that little AID office, and I saw them every time I entered. I remember watching Kennedy's 1961 Inaugural Speech, some two years later, on a film that was available in that same office. How I was stirred by his words, recited with that lilting Boston accent whose tones I can still recall:

"Let the word go forth from this time and place, to friend and
foe alike, that the torch has been passed to a new generation of
Americans - born in this century, tempered by war, disciplined
by a hard and bitter peace, proud of our ancient heritage, and
unwilling to witness or permit the slow undoing of those human
rights to which this nation has always been committed, and to
which we are committed today at home and around the world.
Let every nation know, whether it wishes us well or ill, that
we shall pay any price, bear any burden, meet any hardship,

support any friend, oppose any foe, to assure the survival and the success of liberty.

To those people in the huts and villages of half the globe struggling to break the bonds of mass misery, we pledge our best efforts to help them help themselves, for whatever period is required - not because the communists may be doing it, not because we seek their votes, but because it is right. If a free society cannot help the many who are poor, it cannot save the few who are rich."

Living in Tanganyika, we were at the cutting edge of that struggle. The struggle of the people and huts and villages, as well as the struggle for the hearts and minds of an emerging African population. Nyerere represented a new model for Africa, a model that rejected both the West and the East, which rejected capitalism and communism. It was an exciting vision, a vision that, in retrospect may have been the only way to avoid the tribal strife that came to plague Africa. Even Kenya, considered one of the most stable African countries, is still, today, essentially a tribal based democracy. Unfortunately, Nyerere needed money, and the Chinese were only too happy to cooperate, lending him money, training, advisers, and the full panoply of support. Their influence then, much like their influence in Kenya, Sudan and Angola today, played an important part in Tanzania's demise. Today, as I look at my beloved Kenya, I see the long, sharp fingers of Chinese corruption and greed again playing their role in Africa. Elephants and rhino are being slaughtered for their ivory and the supposed aphrodisiacal quality of their horns, and the Kenya Government turns a blind eye.

Possibly the strongest contributors to my fascination with America were the Americans themselves. They were simply a cut cooler than any of us English kids. They played James Brown (It's a Man's World...) and Tony Joe White, and, later, Hendrix. Part of my fascination for America arose from my friendship with Peter Potter, whose face and features bore a striking resemblance to a white version of Jimi Hendrix, and who danced in a way no other white man I ever knew could dance. His long chin protruded awkwardly, his nose was large, broad, and definitely not WASPy. His hair detonated in a volcanic burst, like an eruption on the sun, uncontrolled and violent. He was also the first person I knew who smoked pot and introduced me to its seduction. His brother, Paul, was effete and languid, more suited to mint julep'd afternoons on a wood-veneered speedboat on Long Island Sound than to the rough-edged cauldron of this mixed race hodge-podge. His father was reputed to be in the CIA. His mother was a redheaded Boston Brahmin who never ventured out of the house while the sun was up. Her bedroom had the first air conditioning machine we had ever seen. America, the land of exotic, fascinating people.

America was, as John F. Kennedy said, "a city upon a hill", and "the eyes of all people" were indeed "upon us." Certainly my eyes and dreams were upon America, even as a teenager, and those dreams became a reality, as dreams tend to do if one harbours them fiercely enough.

CHAPTER 9

Travels in the Levant

1968

I graduated from Ampleforth in December 1967. The English have what is benignly known as a Gap Year. For some the Gap is just that, a black hole of wasted months. But for others, this gap year is a wonderful time for an adventure, to start to define one's own identity. For me, this Gap Year was a time to explore roots, to explore Europe and beyond, to learn who I was and where I fit in the world. In the coming four years of University I would have to decide which way to turn: Would I remain in Kenya and hope for a multi-racial society to develop, one in which the colonial past would be forgotten, erased, and intercourse between races, in all senses, would be the norm? Would I retreat to England, to a class-conscious, urban world with little contact with Nature, the animals and people I had grown to love? Or would I strike out for something new, and what would that be? Other European countries did not seem so hide-bound, but maybe that was just because I was, again, an outsider looking in. Australia and America seemed to offer the best possibilities for a new life, but they were So Far Away. They would represent a huge break from home and family, but, after all, that was part of the colonial tradition. So, this period was the beginning of a search triggered by the instability of Africa and the recognition that the old Colonial world had disappeared.

At seventeen I left the beautiful abbey grounds of Ampleforth for the last time, and made my way by train to Meribel Les Allues, a charming ski resort in the Alps. Several years earlier, aged fourteen, and on my own, I had taken the trains across Europe to find work as a dish washer in a small hotel in this same village, receiving no pay but free board and lodging, a ski pass and the day free to ski. I worked breakfast and dinner and roomed in a tiny bunk bed-ded room with a Yugoslav peasant who was trying to break away from the ethnic problems of his village. During the day I skied, and skied and skied. I made friends with ski patrol members and old instructors who took me under their wing. In the evenings I washed the dishes and collapsed into bed, exhausted and happy, when the last guests retired. That was in 1964. This time I found a youth hostel, shared the room with five other ski bums, and again skied until my legs collapsed.

My parents, however, were intent on me learning Italian, and had booked a course at the Instituto Britanico in Florence, starting in April. So, from April to the end of June I lived in the apartment of Mama Piccini, studied Italian by day, frequented the bars by night, and hitchhiked around Italy on weekends. It was at Mama Piccini's that I met Richard. He arrived one sultry evening in May, wearing a sports jacket, shirt, khaki pants, sensible shoes, and sport-ing a very "public schoolboy"[1] look. His sister had stayed at Mama Piccini's some years earlier and he was also scheduled to attend the Instituto Britanico to study Italian. He was more than a little taken aback to be met at the door by a young man in a kaftan and Indian beads. We became life long friends. At the end of our studies at the Instituto, we decided to hitch hike East. The route was unde-

---

1 English public schools are in fact private, and the equivalent of what would, in America, be considered preppie.

termined, and the timetable non-existent. All that mattered was the journey, and as the Chinese philosopher, Lao Tzu says: *"A good traveler has no fixed plans, and is not intent on arriving."*

Here are four scenes from that journey. Each played a part in forming me and the decisions that I take today.

VENICE

June 28, 1968. The season of lethargy and lassitude was beginning. The air was still and humid. Gondoliers gasped for a cool breeze to ripple the canals. Although the Venetians had not yet fled the city for their annual August absence, the ratio of Venetians to tourists was shifting. Piazza San Marco was filled with Americans, Germans, Japanese and others. We entered the Piazza as the sun was setting, a successful day's hitchhiking from Florence behind us. Long shadows painted the Piazza as couples strolled from the Doge's Palace to the bars that lined the northern edge of the square. On our way in to town, we had found a tourist version of a gondolier's hat. A hard brim and a shallow head area gave it a surprising resemblance to a Frisbee, and as we waited for rides we skimmed the hat back and forth, catching it between our legs, throwing it behind our backs, doing what young men do when they are bored. That evening, hanging out in the Piazza we started to play. Long throws that required a sprint to catch the floating hat; short ones that fluttered and landed gently, permitting the catcher to pose and let the hat descend. Frisbees were barely known in 1968, and certainly even less in Italy. A crowd formed. Our adrenalin and sense of theatre responded, and we played to the crowd. Catching the hat on our heads, skimming it from ground level. Calling on a crowd member to raise his hand and launching the hat to land where he could catch it. Soon enough we were offered drinks and dinner. A delightful middle-aged American couple from Cincinnati, invited us to join them, and, like Marco Polo who had travelled from this same square some seven hundred years earlier, we paid for our dinner with stories of the world beyond. We left that night, stomachs full, heads drowsy, to look for a quiet park where we could lay our heads.

This was the first of many, many times on that trip and others that we were blessed with the generosity of a simple fellow human being. All they asked was the pleasure of conversation, of sharing experiences, of reaching out to another's world. Namaste.

ISTANBUL, TURKEY
July 2 - 5, 1968. The overwhelming impression of Turkey was one of obstreperous, petty bureaucrats. No doubt much of this was attributable to the fact that we were accustomed to the genial Bobby on the English street, carrying his truncheon and a smile, someone with whom you could sit down in a pub and have a pint of beer. By comparison, Turkey in 1968 was Chaos. Decrepit, cold-war era Russian Volgas, "Cars for Comrades", choked the streets, creating a mass of honking, venom-spitting, overheated metal, driven by irate, impatient men. Istanbul was a city in transition, as it has been so many times in the last 2,500 years. Always the cross roads between East and West, now, again, the meeting point of Europe and the Middle East. But, in 1968, it was also the cross roads for a generation of young seekers, pot smokers, disaffected youth. The second phase of the Sexual Revolution. Woodstock, the San Francisco Be-ins, Mr. Tambourine Man were all history. The

second phase involved the East, especially India, and the Road to Katmandu. The Beatles travelled to India in 1968, to Rishikesh where the Maharishi Yogi had his compound. And although transcendental drugs (of the Lucy in the Sky era) were becoming passé, hashish in its various incarnations, was never more popular. Afghanistan, India, Nepal were the places to go.

My friend from Florence, Jenny, had told me to look out for String. He was travelling to Kabul, she told me, and might be in Istanbul about the same time as us. He was tall, very tall, and skinny, with long curly black hair. We would recognize him immediately. Hitching in to Istanbul from the border, Richard and I had to split up. The traffic was almost all Turkish migrant families who worked in Germany and who were returning to Turkey for vacation or to start a new life. Their cars were chock full with family members, furniture and miscellaneous German electronics that they could display to their friends in some rural hamlet in the hinterlands. So hitchhiking was not easy. We had agreed to meet at the "Tent", a legendary hippie hang out, erected on the roof of the Ghulane Hotel overlooking the Blue Mosque, one of Istanbul's most historic sites. It was after midnight when I finally arrived, paid my dinars at the desk below and made my way up the six flights to the roof. Pitch dark. As I stepped hesitatingly through the sleeping bodies, I tripped on one longer than the others. "Sorry, Man. Didn't mean to wake you." "Shit. Find some space and get some sleep." Next morning, as I looked for the man I had woken, I saw a figure taller than anyone I knew, his hair long and curly, his face drawn and gaunt. String. As we talked over a dark Turkish coffee in the Pudding Shop below, Aretha Franklin belting out Respect on the jukebox, he told me his story.

He had been travelling this route for a couple of years. London, Istanbul, Tehran, Kabul, Pakistan and into northern India. Buying artifacts in India and bring them back to London to sell. Of course he smoked hashish along the way, but, he said, he was never a dealer. He never carried drugs across frontiers. Too risky. But this year, entering Turkey, he was stopped at the border and his passport was confiscated. He was driven in to Istanbul where he was unceremoniously deposited in the office of a large, sweaty, unkempt man, in a window office of what appeared to be a Police Headquarters building. A fan creaked near the window, but the 100-degree (Fahrenheit) heat was stifling. The large man rocked in his chair, hair sprouting out of his unbuttoned shirt, chain-smoking the ghastly, pungent Turkish cigarettes. He spoke little English, and let his sidekick, a slender, thin-faced man, who preferred a western style tobacco stick, do the talking. The large man was Big Fies, who, it appeared, was one of the top police officials. Fies told String that he was indefinitely detained in Turkey on suspicion of smuggling drugs, but that his release could be procured if he just cooperated. All he had to do was to sell a quantity of hashish, turn over the proceeds to Fies, and he would be escorted to the eastern border, with passport in hand. String could not give us any assurance that we were not being watched, nor that if we were to take any drugs from him we would be safe. It seemed to him, he said, that the easiest game for Fies to play was to watch the drugs pass from dealer to buyer, arrest the buyer, extract a nice fine, confiscate the drugs and put the whole process back into play. We stayed away.

Later we heard that String had met his quota and moved on, but as naïve 18 year olds, we learned a little about this strange and different world. For centuries Muslims, whether Arab or Persian or Turk, had enjoyed the pleasure of smoking hashish, unfettered by religious or moral scruple. Indeed, since alcohol was prohibited in the Muslim world, the hashish "bars" were often the meeting point for the men of this world. Now, suddenly, the west brought both demand and prohibition. Young people from all over Europe and America were heading east, seeking a new nirvana, often mixed with drugs. But their governments, many of which were closely allied with Turkey, were mandating that drug use be made illegal and stamped out. Where does that leave the police official whose family for generations has seen no harm in the smoking of hashish? He feels no moral urge to participate in the purge, but he quickly sees the economic upside of preying upon the visitors, of enforcing, in a culturally biased way, a law that he felt should apply primarily to the western tourists. Corruption was rampant, an aspect of modern society that was new to us colonial kids. Aretha Franklin blaring opposite the Blue Mosque. Big Feis, the senior policeman enforcing his law, in his very eastern way. The chaos in the streets, built hundreds of years ago for horse and cart, and hastily converted to accommodate the new wealth brought by western investment. All of these were new.

Leaving our privileged enclaves populated by trustworthy friends, we learned that all is not as it seems. Our antennae grew longer and more attentive.

THE GREEK ISLANDS.
July 9 - 12, 1968. Athens was paradise compared to Istanbul. Even the policemen were pleasant. We spent the 3 nights we were in

Athens in the garden of the Temple of Olympian Zeus, close to the Acropolis. Only once were we ejected, and in a most civilized way, by a policeman who was making his rounds about 5.00 in the morning. He directed us to a café that might be open at that hour. Since we had booked a passage on a cargo vessel to Tel Aviv, leaving in a week, and our free accommodation under the stars and the Temple's monumental Corinthian columns was no longer available, we headed to the port of Piraeus, a metro ride from the center of Athens. Walking along the concrete dockside we encountered Kiriakos, a most gentle, affable, owner of a small trawler that ferried heavy objects from island to island. One day it was cement, another it was barrels. Neither of us spoke the other's language, but we understood that we could sleep on his trawler if we would help him load some 6,000 bricks. One day led to the next, and we spent the week unloading product at dawn, motoring to a nearby port during the day, unloading in the late afternoon. As the evening sun fell into the ocean, and the moon arose, the sea became calm and we heard the distant strumming of a lyra or bazouta, a sense of peace, the end of a day's work, time for lamb kebabs with olives, beans, rice, watermelon, and a bottle of Xinomavra red wine. For two tired hitchhikers, this was indeed heaven.

Kiriakos was a happy man. His little black cotton hat, with a short brim that sheltered nothing from the sun, covered a balding head but not much more. Heavy black eyelashes stitched onto his thick, almost corrugated brown skin, protected his sparkling, laughing eyes. He never raised his voice to us, and always greeted us with a smile. One day he complained that we were working too fast, this time unloading oil barrels. Pulling out a vile smelling cigarette, and tapping his well-rounded paunch, he gesticulated to us to sit back and relax against the red and white painted transom of his vessel. On the last evening he invited us to his home in Piraeus to have dinner with his family. We were greeted first by his three children who climbed up his sturdy legs for a hug. Then by his wife, somewhat wider than my particular taste, her hair pulled back into a ponytail under the knot of a red scarf, her feet in flat leather sandals. She fed us fish soup, followed by tomatoes, beans and bread. She smiled, and Kiriakos regaled her with stories of our week, which amused her.

Kiriakos had no toys, but he was, indeed, a happy man. He had the sun to warm him, the sea to soothe him, a family of boisterous children and an attentive wife. He needed no more.

ISRAEL

July 16 – 28, 1968. Our goal was to see Israel and then stow away on a boat from Eilat to Somalia or Ethiopia. After replenishing the calorie count working for a week at Kiryat Anavin, one of Egypt's older Kibbutz, we headed up to Jerusalem. A year earlier, June 5 to 10, 1967, Israel had fought the historic Six Day War, in which, taking their Arab neighbors by surprise, they captured the Sinai desert, the Golan Heights, and the West Bank of Jerusalem, and forced a very rapid capitulation by their enemies. Israel was still jubilant. Troops travelled the main road from Tel Aviv to Jerusalem in high spirits, and Israel was determined to open up its newfound access to the Red Sea, to the Gulf of Aqaba, and the tiny fishing village of Eilat. This was a desolate place at the southern tip of the Negev Desert. No natural reason existed for human life to belong in this deserted stretch of Hades. Searing heat, complete absence of shade, arid winds stirring up the sands of the desert, all awaited the intrepid traveller. But it was through Eilat that we must go to jump ship to Ethiopia or even Somalia.

Arriving at midday in a construction truck that formed part of a military convoy, we were soon reduced to the barely human equivalent of a squeezed washrag. All liquids and even humidity had been wrenched out of us by the incessant and inescapable heat. We had not eaten for two days on the road, and our need for liquids was even more dire. We searched for work in the few hotels that the Israeli government was constructing with an eye to annexing the entire area. Without success. Bottles of water were far beyond our budget, and so we resorted to the ingenious idea of standing below the air conditioning units, with discarded plastic cup in hand, the unit dripping water that it had sucked out of the humid air inside the building. We think of water as being tasteless. But it has a taste, a distinct taste that you can only really enjoy when you have tasted water that has no taste. The absence of any taste. Merely the texture of condensed humidity. But it quenches your thirst. On one such occasion the manager of the hotel whose humid air we were drinking, saw us, took pity on us and offered us work cleaning his huge, refrigerated food storeroom. We cleaned it alright! We left as replete as a trout after a hatch of his favorite flies.

That night we spotted a cargo ship preparing to depart, and were able to smuggle ourselves on board unnoticed. We slid quietly into a lifeboat, unfastened the cover and slipped surreptitiously inside. Oh what expectation. In a few hours we would be underway, and then, with dawn breaking we would announce our presence and offer to work for food. Ethiopia in two days and then on to Kenya. As darkness enveloped us, and we fell into an exhausted sleep, we were smiling. But, our hopes were dashed around midnight when a night guard discovered us (we had left loose the rope that tied down the cover) and dumped us out on the dock.

Our adventure had come to an end, but during the course of less than a month we had learned more patience, ability to tolerate reversal, hunger, and absence, and above all, the joy of "dancing beneath a diamond sky with one hand waving free . . .",[m] living each day as it came. I have never owned, or possessed, less material goods. We were indeed penniless. I believe that I have never needed to possess more than the confidence, exuberance and desire to experience new worlds, that we had on that first trip.

---

m   Bob Dylan: *Mr. Tambourine Man.*

CHAPTER 10

DISCOVERING KENYA

1969

In 1969, after the summer of this first hitchhiking expedition, and during my first months at University, my parents moved back to Kenya. Tanzania had taken a turn toward socialism, while Kenya had embraced the West with open arms. Alan was offered the post of Managing Director of a group of East African newspapers owned by the English conglomerate, Lonrho. Our future clearly lay in Kenya. While I had been born in Kenya, in 1950, I had no memories of that country, so this was a new experience for me.

The summer of 1969, arriving in Nairobi, and for several summers afterwards during the University years, I worked as a driver and guide for Church Safaris, an outfit dedicated to safaris in the Kenyan wilderness, which broke the mold of the traditional game park routes. Instead of staying in lodges, we drove our Land Rovers to remote locations and pitched camp. Instead of looking for wild game from the insulated bubble of a Minibus, we rode horses, we hiked, and we slept around campfires. Occasionally, as we slept in tents by a watering hole in Tsavo, we would hear elephant walking and grazing yards from our tent. They must have known we were there, and we knew that they knew that we were there. But we were not troubling them and they were happy to let us be part of their environment.

Tony Church's major client was the Sierra Club, and, once again, I was exposed to Americans. Admittedly, it was to those Americans who could afford to come to Africa in the late '60s, and who were interested in a more rustic, environmentally pure experience. They may have been the tip of the iceberg. But they were the tip that I saw, and just as in the earlier years in Tanganyika, I felt drawn to visit their land.

Fortunately Church's Safaris left time for other activities. My closest friend was Dave Harries, the son of an Anglican priest, and, like the proverbial "son of a preacher man", Dave knew how to have fun. We both loved to fish and to explore remote parts of Kenya, so it was no surprise when we decided to pack his Land Rover and set off on a Kenya Road Trip.

Mount Kenya

The first time I was exposed to mountains was when, at 19 years old, Dave and I climbed the Lenana Peak of Mount Kenya. Mount Kenya rises steeply from the highlands of central Kenya. The vegetation in the foothills is lush and forested. Juniper trees grow to over a hundred feet. Red-hot pokers, violets and giant forest lobelia are prolific on the lower slopes. But as you rise above 12,000 feet only the lobelia and the irrepressible grass tussocks survive the needle ice that forms at night and penetrates all living beings.

In those days there was no trail, as such, just a general sense of the direction of the mountain. The first day we trudged through soggy marshland, thick with a kind of heather which sometimes supported one's weight, but which often squished into the boggy terrain below. We wore simple hiking boots with plastic bags covering our socks. In retrospect, we were woefully unprepared. No dry change of clothes. Sleeping bags designed for the Kenyan velt, not for nights at 15,000 feet. Jeans and woolen underwear. One would shudder at the thought of such an ill equipped expedition today.

After slogging through the muddy bracken for a day, we reached a flattish area dotted with small lakes, known as tarns. Nestled at the feet of the rocky crags that spiked upwards, the three peaks, Batian, Lenana and Nelion, there are tarns of an unfathomable depth, and an exceptional clarity. Here we saw lammergeirs and Verreaux's eagle (preying on the rock hyrax, a rat-like animal, about the size of a marmot, that is the closest living relative to the elephant). Many decades earlier, Colonel Grogan and a group of Scottish settlers had introduced brown trout to these tarns, and without natural predators, but plenty of bug life, they had flourished. Dave and I took our "smuggler's rods" - simple fishing rods with four breaks instead of the usual one break in the middle – out of their cloth cases, and set about fishing for dinner. Nothing tastes quite as good as fresh brown trout cooked with herbs in tin foil on an open fire with the three majestic peaks of a spiritual mountain looming around you.

The night was miserably cold, and though we wore everything we had and dug ourselves deep into our sleeping bags, we barely slept a wink. At 3.00 am we rose and started the ascent of Lenana peak. For those of you not accustomed to mountains, this early morning rise is commonplace. The mountaintop air is usually clearest at first light, rewarding those who reach the summit at daybreak. Later in the day clouds roll in, rain or snow is often encountered. And, of course, if you can stand at the summit at daybreak you have the additional pleasure of the sunrise. You can watch the Hunter cast his noose, capturing first the neighboring peaks, then painting gold the walls of rock, and finally creating long shadows that stretch like a pianist's fingers across the plain below.

We reached the summit just as dawn was breaking. The sense of excitement and accomplishment was more than just invigorating. It was palpable. It seemed to us that all of Africa stretched out below us. In the distance we could just make out the peak of Mount Kilimanjaro. As we hugged each other on the summit, Dave told me he would never leave Kenya. He loved the land, the people, the wild life, and the proximity to the pulse of the earth. We agreed to return to climb Kilimanjaro, and another African seed was sown in my soul. Dave died in 2012 leading a group of young Kenyans up Mount Kenya. He could not have died in a better way: he loved children and he loved Mount Kenya. I miss his toothless grin.

Dave was clear about who he was. He was a Kenyan. His family had been missionaries, and so they never belonged to that white settler tribe who resisted change. Instead, his father, the Pastor of the Anglican Church in Nairobi, was close to his largely African congregation. Charles Njonjo, the Attorney General of Kenya, was a close friend, and was Dave's godfather. Race meant nothing to Dave. He was as happy sitting with a group of Kikuyu elders in a makeshift bar in the Aberdare mountains, drinking a beer and making friends, as he was sipping gin and tonics by a pool in an upscale tourist resort. He played club rugby with a mixed race team in Nairobi (as did my brother in law, Charlie). He supported the Kenya athletes as they began to make their mark on the runners' world. It is interesting to note that no Kenyan won a medal in the Olympic games until after Independence, and that only three Kenyans had even completed in the Olympics before Independence. It is little wonder that Kenyan identity, especially for whites, was barely in its infancy even as late as 1969. Dave was part of that first generation of whites that felt Kenyan. His sense of identity was infectious. With Dave Harries, I grew comfortable saying "I'm from Kenya" when people asked, but I was not yet ready to say "I'm Kenyan." If I was Kenyan, what was my tribe? I was certainly not comfortable being identified with the tribe of white settlers. And obviously I was not Luo or Kikuyu or Kalenjin. Being "from" Kenya seemed like a reasonable compromise position.

TURKANA AND THE RENDILLE

From the slopes of Mount Kenya, Dave, Angela (who later became Dave's wife), Jenny (my friend from Florence) and I headed north to Samburu and Isiolo, and thence west to Marsabit, all part of the Northern Frontier of Kenya. This area stretches from the coast along the border with Ethiopia and Sudan until Kenya meets with Uganda at Lake Turkana, the Jade Sea. It is an arid, desolate, inhospitable land. Mostly it is flat scrub grassland that receives little rain. In places it is just endless rocks interspersed with salty sand. The wind dances across its surface like a djinn, grabbing handfuls of sand and scattering them to blow hither and yon. Occasionally it forms tiny tornados that spin like helicopter blades and torment the animals. It is home to several subspecies not found anywhere else in the world: Grevy's zebra, the reticulated giraffe, Besia Oryx and Somali Ostrich are some of the species we wished to encounter.

At Marsabit you come to a jewel of a game park, a forest in the desert. Here roamed Ahmed, the iconic patriarchal elephant whose tusks were more than six feet long, who was individually designated as a national treasure, and whose tusks are now proudly displayed in the National Museum in Nairobi. But, leaving Marsabit headed further west, the desert becomes completely arid, flat, white and salty, the dry remains of an evaporated ocean. There are no roads, no paths, just compass bearings to lead one to Lake Turkana. This desert is the land of the Rendille, who, for the reasons I will describe, are, to my mind, the Lost Tribe of Israel.

The rain clouds that form over the Indian Ocean and blow west across the Chalbi desert of the Northern frontier, progress unimpeded for some three hundred miles. Then, without warning, some thirty miles from Lake Turkana, there is a protrusion, the remains of the western edge of a long eroded volcano, a hill some 7,500 feet high, and some six miles long, known as Mount Kulal. The rain clouds hit Kulal and mercilessly dump rain twice a year during the monsoons. The topography of Mount Kulal creates what is known as orographic lifting: air masses are forced from lower to higher elevation, where they cool down and thus can no longer hold as much moisture, so that clouds and precipitation form. It is a dense forest, an island of luxuriant humidity in the midst of an ocean of parched soil. And it is teeming with elephant, buffalo, colobus monkeys, and other forest life, some of which are unique to that forest because it has been cut off from the rest of the world for eons.

As we navigated our way up a rutted path, we came across a remote and tiny mission church. In conversation with the missionary priest that afternoon, we learned that the next day was a special day, and that it would behoove us to spend the night and the next morning by a *manyatta* located at the foot of Mount Kulal. A *manyatta* is like a compound. Semi-nomadic peoples, like the Rendille and the Maasai, build their huts in a small area and surround the area with thorn bush, creating a wall around the compound similar in style and height to that of a roll of barbed wire fencing. This thorn bush wall serves to keep lions, hyenas and other predators out of the *manyatta* at night, and to keep goats and cattle safe from these carnivores. Each family lives in its own hut, the goats sleeping inside the hut with the family, and cows tethered outside.

We camped by a *wadi*, near the *manyatta*, and awaited the dawn. As the sun rose, little boys aged six and seven led the goats out to feed. Some older girls tended to the camels. The elders gathered under an acacia tree nearby, their women prepared heavily sweetened tea for the men, and a few of the men who spoke Swahili approached us inquisitively. Around 8.00 a.m. the boys returned with the goats, and the one Somali family who travelled with this Rendille group were asked to leave the *manyatta* and joined us on the edge of the *wadi* to watch the proceedings.

The *manyatta* became a hive of activity. It was the beginning of the celebration of Soriyo, which occurs twice a year. Previously unseen women emerged from their huts. The multitude of children stopped running here and there, and gathered with their parents and grandparents in an open space in the center of the *manyatta*. An elder led a large goat, possibly the largest there was, to the center of this group and tied him to a stake in the ground. A small hole, about the size of a baobab seed gourd, was dug in the hard ground, and the elder swiftly, with little ado, slit the throat of the unsuspecting animal. Blood squirted out, was caught in gourds or flowed into the hole in the ground. Promptly, each male head of family dipped his forefinger into the blood and marked the sign of a cross on his forehead. Following this ritual, each family retired to a spot in front of their own hut, slaughtered a young goat, a kid, and went through the same ritual marking of the forehead or chest, but on each member of the family, and then marked the area above the entryway to the hut with the blood of the goat. Many families also marked their camels with a cross on the camel's hump. Finally, small fires were lit and the families feasted on the meat of the kid.

The Rendille are a tall people, slender and Nilotic in appearance. Their noses long and thin, their cheek bones high and pronounced. They are semi nomadic herders in the tradition of the early Jews. They speak a Cushitic language. They clearly have no kinship with the smaller, agrarian Bantu people, like the Kikuyu and the Embu who populate central Kenya. Their stature and physiognomy is more akin to the Samburu and Maasai. Studies of their DNA, and their oral folk history both suggest that they migrated south from Egypt through Ethiopia and down to this arid land millennia ago. This history links them with the Falashas, a Jewish sect of Ethiopians, whom they resemble physically (and who claim lineage from the Queen of Sheba). I like to think that these factors and the ceremony we witnessed all tie the Rendille to ancient Jewish peoples and to the biblical Lost Tribe of Israel.

From Kulal we travelled on to Lake Turkana, as remote a place as one is likely to find anywhere. The Turkana people are blacker than the spray of a squid, more rugged than rocks hewn from tectonic shifts, and renowned for their fierceness. The men wear only a loin cloth with one end wrapped over the shoulder, and carry a strong walking stick, a razor sharp blade (*abarait*) in the form of a bracelet sheathed in goat skin around their wrist, and a small wooden headrest (*ekicholong*) on which they lay their heads when they wish to sleep. In their lower lips the men, especially elders, insert wooden plugs that can hang some two to three inches from the mouth. Often they will carry some kind of spiked instrument stuck into their hair. Finally, the men often accentuate their fierce look by capping their hair with a clay mixture which they dye a blue grey and then weave ostrich feathers into the clay "headpiece".

The women wear a leather wrap around their waist garlanded with ostrich and other shells. Many of them also wear bands of copper and tin around their necks, sometimes as many as six or seven, giving their necks an elongated look. Below that, resting on their chest, they wear beaded necklaces, similar to those worn by Maasai women, but less flat, and also necklaces made from ostrich shells cut into little circular pieces the size of a small coin.

The Turkana tend cattle and live off the land. They share access to Lake Turkana with the Molo people, a gentler, fishing people who stay out of the way of the Turkana. The Molo build little rafts about five feet long and the width of three doum palm tree trunks. The men head out every day into the lake, standing with consummate skill on these precarious platforms, paddling with a long wooden stick. They are also armed with a spear, and when they see a fish they are able, quite miraculously, to spear the fish from a standing position. Whacking it on the head they leave it in the raft, where, covered by the water that flows between the trunks, the fish remains fresh. This form of subsistence is not without its risks because they share the lake with a large population of crocodiles who also enjoy a good meal of Nile perch or tilapia, and who, from time to time also upset the rafts and dine on the more succulent food that falls into the lake.

I was not aware of this last fact when, on meeting my first Molo fisherman, I signaled to him that I would like to join him on his expedition. After some minutes of sign language negotiation, I agreed to give him my blue and white striped swimsuit in return for the pleasure of accompanying him as he fished. It was a wonderful experience, and a fair trade. The only problem was that he demanded payment in advance, and those parts of me that had not been accustomed to daily sun became quite badly burned. Today the Molo people are dying out. By most counts, the tribe now numbers less than four hundred members. They will soon be assimilated, and their particular customs, like my swimsuit, will be a thing of the past.

Road trips in Africa take on a different dimension. If one chooses to take the "road less travelled", as we often did on this trip, one is constantly surprised. On our way back from Turkana, we decided to drive through the Matthews range of mountains. About noon, with the sun beating down a stifling 42 degrees centigrade, there was a loud bang, or series of bangs, the car shuddered and Dave pulled to a halt. "Puncture!" he proclaimed as he turned off the ignition. Opening the door he looked forward, looked back, then leapt out of the Land Rover and emitted a great curse. As he walked around the Land Rover, his cursing increased. All four tires had simultaneously been punctured. Not by glass, but by some perilously powerful thorns scattered across the path, probably the remains of a *manyatta* thorn fence erected and removed some nights before. Angela, ever the serene one, unpacked a *kikapu*, or woven reed bag, sat in it, using the side to support her back, and rolled a couple of joints. Taking a filter tipped cigarette she emptied out all the tobacco. She rubbed the marijuana plant against a small colander until only a fine dust settled through the holes of the colander. This she poured back into the filtered cigarette. "Time to chill" she said, as she drew a long drag. Then she set about making a pot of hot tea to equalize the temperature within and without our bodies, an old remedy for countering blistering heat. Dave and I jacked up the entire vehicle, one corner at a time, resting its axles and framework on large stones, removed each wheel, patched the tires and gradually got the car back to drive-able condition. The whole process must have taken two hours. But there was no hurry, we had no place we had to be, and this, like all the rest of the trip, was part of the experience.

That night we camped in the Matthews range, a range of mountains without a road to be seen, but plenty of elephant tracks. We decided, on the advice of a young Samburu warrior to whom we had given a ride, to follow an elephant track across a pass in the mountains. In the morning we set out early, Dave driving, Jenny sitting next to him in front, and Angela and I perched in the spare tire that was affixed to the bonnet of the Land Rover. Dave drove slowly, carefully, following the elephant path at walking speed. The one thing we had was time ... and freedom, of course. As Kris Kristofferson sang, about freedom: it "ain't worth nothing, but its free."[n] In an atypical moment of lack of concentration, Dave hit a huge rut. The right front wheel disappeared into a small crevasse, and Angela was hurled forward in front of the car. She landed on her wrist, cracking several bones. Angela was a tough Kenya girl. We tied a splint using the thigh bone of some animal, probably some form of antelope, to hold her hand and wrist in shape, and soldiered on to the end of the pass where we encountered a

---

n   Kris Kristofferson: *Me and Bobby McGee.*

convent of Irish nuns who helped treat Angie's growing pain and discomfort.

Later that summer I travelled to Lamu. In Lamu, time is not measured in years or decades, or even centuries. That measure of time has stood still since long before Marie Antoinette lost her pretty head to revolutionaries, before Handel composed his Alleluia chorus, even before the Pilgrims landed on Plymouth Rock. Lamu is frozen in Time, like a dinosaur fossil, unchanged for centuries, but with its heart, its lungs, its organs intact and beating. The clock that ticks in Lamu is the ebb and flow of the tides, high tide and low tide; the waxing and waning of the moon, full moon bringing higher high tides and lower low tides; the breathing of the winds, the strong coastal winds that blow in every afternoon and then rest at night breathing softly into the bedroom windows set on the highest floors of Lamu's elegant Arab homes; and the feeding cycle of the fish whose protein fuels the energy of the people but also demands their assiduous attention and labor. There is indeed, in Lamu, a "time and tide in the affairs of men", but it is not the time or tide that Shakespeare referred to or that we know in the West.

Lamu is an island off the northeastern coast of Kenya. When the Sultans of Oman, and before them the early Saudi traders, plied their wares from India to Madagascar, Lamu, like Zanzibar, was one of the ports at which they rested, traded and restocked their pantries. During the 1600s, these Arab traders built elaborate homes, mosques, and market places, all of which survive and are central to the life of this unique island today.

Today one can fly to a nearby airstrip on the mainland. Forty years ago the only access was by dhow from Mombasa or Malindi, or by bus along the mainland and a spray swept ride in an *ngalawa* across the bay to the island. I travelled to Lamu by bus from Malindi, a trip of some fourteen hours. Like most African transport, the bus carried not just people and their suitcases, but their goats, their chickens, and a bevy of snotty nosed children perched on the lap of an already overburdened mother. Every hour or so the bus stopped at, or near, some remote village. In the bigger villages women appeared like a swarm of worker ants, laden with their wares for sale: bananas, coconuts, doum palm baskets, coral necklaces, cowrie shell bracelets. If you descended from the bus you were overwhelmed by these insect-like creatures, and had to resist the urge to swat at them like flies. Taking a stroll was impossible as the crowd thronged closer than paparazzi on a rock star. If you stayed in the bus, arms would stretch up to the window offering tastes of the fruit and samples of the jewelry. The bus driver's assistant yelled and gesticulated at all and sundry, and then leaped to the roof attaching baskets, handbags, even animals precariously perched atop the rickety old warhorse of a bus. Finally, with bodies still hanging to rails and windows, the bus crashed into gear, emitted a foul cloud of diesel-filled smoke, and started off down the road, leaving the disappointed crowd to wait for another day, another busload of passengers.

Other stops were more peaceful. Several rivers crossed our path. In some, mere streams, the passengers were evacuated and the bus, with plenty of verbal assistance and some pushing, pulling, leaning and shoving, negotiated its way across. At Garsen we crossed the Tana River by ferry, just long enough to fit the bus and its passengers who stood expectantly beside the bus as it carefully inched its way onto the ferry. At that stage, all male hands were put to work since the ferry was powered only by the men pulling on the rope that ran from shore to shore and through some eyes and pulleys on the ferry. A chant emerged, and strong black shoulders glistened in the sun as they heaved on the rope like sailors raising the mainsail.

Today there is a fifty-person ferry that runs from the mainland to Lamu Island and town. Like so many third world ferries, it has had its share of accidents, including a recent capsize New Years Day 2012, when it was overloaded with eighty passengers and hit another boat in the dark. But in 1970, lateen sailed, single outrigger *ngalawas*, and the occasional small motor driven fishing boats were the only option. As I stepped out of the *ngalawa* onto the lowest step of the wall of the long Lamu waterfront, I was transported back four hundred years. I stepped through a C.S. Lewis-like cupboard into the past. Time, as we know it, evaporated.

It's 9.30 in the morning. The sun is not burning, the breeze is light, and the tide is three hours from high. In two days it will be full moon, so the flow of water into the Lamu channel is strong, the water level rising almost two feet in an hour, and the flow in mid channel running many yards a minute. The waterfront is a hive of activity. The larger dhows, *jahazis*, which line the waterfront, anchored in a foot of water at low tide, or even resting on their shallow keels, are now riding in six feet of water. If they have not been loaded by now, with mangrove trunks, barrels of oil, sesame seeds or cement, their crew are working desperately to load the last pieces before the tide gets too high. The captains of the smaller boats, the *ngalawas*, are sitting drinking a sweet milky tea, or cajoling a donkey to make way for them. Their workday has not started. They are fishermen. They have not yet unfurled their sails, as they wait for the breeze to pick up and for the strongest flood tide to pass. There is a little more than twelve hours between high tide and low tide, and in that time, when the moon is full and the volume of water moving with the tide is greatest, the water will rise and fall as much as twelve feet. The volume of water ebbing or flowing changes like a bell curve, in the first and last two hours as little as six inches an hour, but in the sixth and seventh hours, as much as two feet an hour. With the light morning breeze and the strong tide flow, these *ngalawas* cannot make headway out of the channel, but in two hours or so, the breeze will stiffen, the tide flow will diminish, and they will set off to fish for the evening catch.

The waterfront is also the main avenue. It is the only place wide enough for a car to pass, but there are no cars other than one Land Rover owned by the District Commissioner. There are not even any motorbikes. All transportation is by donkey. Behind the façade of the waterfront, Lamu is an ant nest of tiny alleyways, wide enough for a loaded donkey to pass, but not for two to pass in opposite directions. I wander in from the waterfront to find my lodging, the New Mahrus Hotel. It is in the center of town. At six stories, it is one of the tallest buildings on the island, with magnificent views from its flat balconied roof. It is populated by *jahazi* captains seeking company and a bed while their boat is in port a few nights, by Swahili businessmen and traders from the mainland, and, camped out on the roof, a smattering of young white travellers, some of them Kenyans, others visitors from Germany, France and the Netherlands, mostly long haired and seeking that timelessness that Lamu offers.

Walking to the New Mahrus, I cross the town's main square. Set in front of a large fort built by the Omanis in 1821, the square is shaded by two enormous Indian almond trees. It is nearly midday as I sit on a bench under one of the trees, next to two ancient

Swahili gentlemen discussing the politics of the town. Even though the sun has risen and sits high above us, uncovered by clouds or buildings, the day is yet fresh. The midday breeze is beginning, and with it the palms begin to sway, the leaves of the almond trees ripple above us, and the cotton dresses that cover the women flap playfully about. Young boys smack the rumps of donkeys carrying everything from wood or coral for building, to baskets of fruit en route to a market, to cases of soft drink that can be purchased as the donkeys walk dolefully through the narrow streets. Other boys, a few years older, pull carts or guide donkeys dragging mangrove trunks to the waterfront to be loaded onto *jahazis* and shipped to Mombasa or points beyond. Sacks of coconuts or sesame lie carelessly scattered on the ground in the shade of the broad branched trees. Women, dressed from head to toe in black, with pretty decorated little shoes and hennaed toes pass statuesquely through the square bearing bags or pots on their heads. Three women stop to chat. All I can see are their feet, their hands, also hennaed, and their eyes, flashing from beneath their *bui-buis*. But even with this tantalizingly limited exposure, I can make out one girl whose grace and beauty are staggering. Her skin is a light coffee color, her hands delicate, her fingers long. Her eyes are bright, outlined with kohl. They sparkle as she speaks. She raises her hand to her mouth as she giggles at the story her friend is recounting. Silver bracelets ring her wrists. Do they talk of glances exchanged in passageways, of the sighing of a well muscled fisherman as she walks by, or is their exchange less light, maybe laden with the prescience of an arranged marriage to a wealthy island sheik? The girls don't linger long to chat, and certainly they don't rest under the almond tree, which appears to be reserved for men.

In search of lunch I make my way back to the waterfront. The activity has changed. The boats are all fully laden. Many have set sail. On others, the sailors and fishermen are hauling sisal ropes through creaking pulleys to raise the yard of their lateen-rigged sails. The breeze is now brisk. White caps top the waves as spray spumes leeward. The earlier calm is replaced by an urgency as the combination of high tide and a mounting breeze beats the water against the wall of the waterfront with a frothing, pulsing, turbulent energy. Sails flap; unsecured ropes crack and whip; captains shout orders. The day is in its glory.

I stroll up the front. I pass the boat makers, carving great beams that will serve as the spine of a *jahazi,* and others shaping the cross planks. The noise of their hammers seems to beat in rhythm with the crashing of the waves against the waterfront wall. There are bed makers, and door carvers, basket weavers and sail makers. I stop to ask Omar how he learned to build *jahazi*, and, not unexpectedly, he tells me that he learned from his father, who in turned learned from his father. The skill has been in the family for generations. I wonder how many. Could it be that four hundred years ago one of Omar's ancestors sat on this very shore carving wood to build sailing vessels? Entirely possible.

Later that afternoon, as the sun is falling into the ocean, I walk east along the shoreline. The shore is impassable at high tide and for an hour or two either side of high tide, depending on the moon. But, by 4.00 p.m. the tide has ebbed some six feet, and, picking my way through mangrove trees, then crossing a corral strewn stretch of beach, I come to the beach that begins Shela town, and beyond, the miles of sand dunes that front the Indian Ocean. I walk out for nearly an hour, passing pools of receding water that leave little crabs and invertebrates scurrying for shelter. Climbing up a dune to watch the sun settle gently into the Kenyan mainland I see camels in the distance. The breeze has subsided. The fishermen in their *ngalawas* are returning home, their catches fresh for the evening meal. As the sun falls, orange and red, into the ocean, the muezzin chant the sunset prayer. Five times a day, starting before sunrise, the chant of the muezzin can be heard all across the island from the myriad of mosques, small and large, that dot this beautiful island. The pre-dawn chant, *Isha,* is my daily wake up call, its rhythmic beauty stirring me from slumber. *"Hayya 'ala al-salaah, hayya 'ala al-falaah"* calls the muezzin, "come to prayer, come to prosperity." But this evening, the *Mahgrib,* or evening prayer, is yet more deeply moving as I sit cross legged on a high dune, the breeze skipping softly across the waves breaking on the miles of untouched sand, fanning my face, lifting my spirit, and filling my soul with awe at the endless, effortless beauty of Nature.

CHAPTER 11

CAIRO TO NAIROBI OVERLAND

1971

Before Richard and I graduated from University, some three years after our first trip, we travelled again. The first time had been during our gap year, barely out of high school, no hair upon the face, and without a penny to our names. This time we were close to finishing University. Our path was more directed. We had saved some money delivering flowers to the exclusive SW1 addresses in London during Christmas, and could afford to pay the fare for the occasional public transport. We wanted to get to Kenya overland, spending little and seeing the world. In the gap year we had been feathers on the wind. We set out to join the trail to Kathmandu, but found ourselves in Greece and Israel. This time we had our route planned. We hitched through Europe in two days and caught a boat from Naples to Alexandria, in Egypt. From there the plan was up the Nile, into Sudan, and on to Kenya through the upper reaches of Uganda and Murchison falls.

This time we had Kris Kristofferson's all time Road Song, Me and Bobby McGee on our brains:

Busted flat in Baton Rouge, headin' for the trains,
Feelin' nearly faded as my jeans.
Bobby thumbed a diesel down just before it rained,

Took us all the way to New Orleans.
Took my harpoon out of my dirty red bandana
And was blowin' sad while Bobby sang the blues,
With them windshield wipers slappin' time and
Bobby clappin' hands we finally sang up every song
That driver knew.

Freedom's just another word for nothin' left to lose,
And nothin' ain't worth nothin' but it's free,
Feelin' good was easy, Lord, when Bobby sang the blues,
And buddy, that was good enough for me,
Good enough for me and my Bobby McGee.

Here are four vignettes from that second trip.

EGYPT

July 1971. We had a friend in the Egyptian Embassy in London who told us that women's underwear from Marks & Spencer's was the rage in Cairo, and that if we smuggled it in he had a contact who would buy it from us. We travelled ridiculously light by today's standards. No backpack. The shorts and shirt we wore, a pair of jeans, a clean shirt, and about 25 books. We carried a small suitcase, the size of a modern woman's handbag, and in it we stuffed all the bras, panties and other undergarments we could squeeze in there. It was a miracle that we passed through customs. I suppose we carried so little that no one could have imagined us with such contraband.

Arrive in Cairo. Call the contact. She is in Alexandria for a week. Well, a week is a long time when you are hitchhiking, especially when you have limited funds and have to find accommodation in a city. No alternative. We have to sell them ourselves. But how? You can't exactly stand in Tahrir Square hawking illegal goods (purchased in a Jewish-owned store, no less). Investigate various women's retail stores, but none carry underwear, at least not visibly. Maybe Egyptian women don't wear underwear, we speculate. No, there has to be a middle class group of ladies who aspire to such finery, but who do not have the funds to travel and purchase such luxuries. Brainstorm. The waitresses at the Hilton. They dress nicely, are exposed to western women and styles, have some disposable cash, but not enough to travel.

8.00 a.m. Friday, July 9, 1971. Islam's holy day, so not much commerce. Two scruffy, longhaired young men sitting in the Hilton coffee shop. Waitress approaches. Quite tall. Definitely attractive. Speaks English. She takes our order. We crack open the suitcase and ask her, surreptitiously, if she is interested in buying some underwear. Eyes brighten under the layer of kohl that she is wearing. Looking around with a hunted air she tells us to follow her back into the kitchen. Chaos erupts. Within minutes we are surrounded by waitresses, grabbing, sizing, comparing, babbling in tongues. Although we are somewhat overwhelmed, Richard and I are adrenalized by the surge of entrepreneurial success. No doubt about it, the product is a success and we have identified the target market. And no middlemen. Well, not quite, because at that moment the manager approaches, shouting loudly and rapidly at the waitresses about why aren't they in the restaurant, the customers are waiting etc. Clearly this calls for some delicate maneuvering. Fortunately we had a couple of M&S t–shirts which we offered him. He told us to return at 11.00 when the place was empty, and we could continue our sales effort. The mark-up was on average over 500%. We left with our pockets filled with Egyptian currency, which, we soon discovered, had to be spent in Egypt, and was not convertible. Richard bought his girlfriend an alexandrite ring (probably synthetic) and I bought a pair of silver fighting cocks (definitely not silver, probably pewter). And we spent the rest on hiring a pair of horses to ride out to the pyramids.

SUDAN

Travelling south from Egypt, one enters Sudan at Wadi Halfa, a desolate, barren, end of the line kind of town. Here one disembarks from whatever water-born transport you have enjoyed in Egypt, and are faced with the prospect of two days and nights in a train to Khartoum. Or, if you are very poor, on the roof of a train to Khartoum.

The tracks had been laid in the 1890's by Lord Kitchener as he campaigned to rescue British pride from the murder of General Gordon by the Mahdi in Khartoum, and had not been updated since. The train had four classes of service. Fourth class was on the flat roof of the train, with nothing but a railing to prevent you from rolling off into the endless kilometers of desert, and a ladder from the roof down to the 3ʳᵈ class compartment below. Average temperatures in northern Sudan in July are over 41 Centigrade (105 Fahrenheit) and the journey is essentially a curve-less, flat shot, straight across the southern flank of the Sahara desert. Toilet facilities were non-existent for this class of travel, so, when nature called, one simply descended as far as possible down the ladder, hung one's backside out in the breeze, and answered nature's call. Toilet paper was not provided, but we had come armed with a small library of books. I was midway through *The Beastly Beatitudes of Balthazar B*, by the great Irish writer, J. P. Donleavy. Nature called me not once, but twice, that first night, and the pages of Balthazar B were called into service. Not to worry I thought, Richard has already read it and I can put the first chapters to good use. Alas, as morning broke, I realized my mistake. I had torn my toilet paper from the back of the book, not the front, and I never did finish Balthazar's Beastly Beatitudes.

Khartoum: Capital city of Sudan. Junction of the Blue and White Niles. Since time immemorial Sudan has been riven by conflict between the Arab northerners and the African southerners. For most of the decades after independence, Sudan was ruled by military men of Arab descent. In 1969, General Nimeri, a colonel in the army, joined with other officers and, in a bloodless coup, took control of the government. Immediately he faced opposition from incipient communist groups and from radical Islamists, and his grip on the reins of power was tentative.

July 20, 1971. Together with about 20 other dishevelled travellers, Richard and I were asleep in the youth hostel on the outskirts of Khartoum. At about 2 a.m. we were awoken by the sounds of bombs, rocket fire and grenades. The airport was next to the hostel, and a communist group had captured Nimeri and taken power. As part of their coup, they also captured the airport, the radio station, and several key military posts. Nimeri was imprisoned in the Presidential Palace.

Given the proximity to the airport, the hostel was closed and its shabby polyglot inmates were evicted. Each went to their embassy for shelter. The Germans and French were welcomed into their embassies and given temporary lodging. The Americans fared even better. They were invited to some kind of belated July 4 party, and got to eat and drink in the elegant marble hallways, play Frisbee in the shaded embassy gardens, and mingle with the nubile daughters of CIA undercover agents. Richard and I duly showed up at the British Embassy and pled our case for shelter. After all, we were British citizens caught in the midst of an armed revolution. An Under-Secretary met us, offered us a cup of tea, and dismissed us with: "Well you know where we are chaps. Let us know if you run into any trouble."

"Trouble," I thought, "what the hell is Trouble if it does not include being caught in the cross fire of a revolution?" But, with those encouraging words, we stepped out onto Jamhouriyah Street and started to wander. As we wandered, a boy approached us. He was a few years younger than us, and, like third world youth all over the planet, seemed eager to try out his English. Our patience for someone trying to sell us drugs, fighting cocks or alexandrite jewelry was zero, but something struck us about this boy, who seemed less pushy, more sincere than the others. And so it was that we met the son of one of the very few Jewish families remaining in Sudan at the time. He said his father was the Rabbi, and he let us stay in the synagogue. We never met the father, nor any family member other than Ezra, but we slept on the pews of the synagogue for the four days that the revolution lasted. Tanks roaming openly and threateningly, an ominous absence of Sudanese in the streets, and deafening silence on the radio, all did not bode well for the revolution. And, indeed, just 4 days later, Nimeri escaped by jumping out of the window of his jail, rallied his men and overthrew the clearly hapless communists. We got out of Sudan as quickly as we could.

ETHIOPIA

Axum is one of the oldest towns in Ethiopia, and is home to an ancient Coptic Christian cathedral, St. Mary of Zion. Dark black, bearded men in long white robes populate the grounds, and while away the day in the shade of the broad-branching sycamore trees. Gossip, hand-holding, camaraderie, but no action. Just the enjoyment of the company of friends, possibly a cup of tea and a sweet pastry. No women are anywhere to be seen because this is a Holy place. It is the place where the Ark of the Covenant rests, brought here by the Emperor Menelik I from Egypt where he had gone to visit his father, King Solomon, and his mother, the Queen of Sheba in about 950 B.C.

As we approached, there was a stirring among the white robed elders. Conversations were cut short. Gesticulating hands stopped gesticulating and began pointing, pointing at us. Then a flurry of elders ran up to us, yelling, waving wildly, making signs for us to stop in our tracks. The problem, it transpired, was that, with our long shaggy hair and slender, maybe even emaciated, physiques, we were mistaken for women, and women were absolutely NOT allowed in the church grounds. At that moment I am struck by memories of Achilles, dressed as a girl and dancing for Ulysses with the daughters of Lycomedes. When we finally showed irrefutable proof of our gender, there was great mirth and laughter. We were welcomed generously, and shown around by an elder who spoke enough Italian for us to communicate hesitatingly.

Axum is the northern-most town on the highway from Eritrea, in the north, to Gondar, Bahar Dar and Addis Ababa in the South. In 1971, the peoples of northern Ethiopia, or Eritrea, were fighting for their independence, and it was just our luck, once again, to be thrust into the middle of conflict. We had travelled from Jerusalem to Eilat as part of a military convoy. We had been ejected from the hostel in Khartoum to walk the tank-filled streets following the Communist revolution. Now we were to ride in trucks with bullet-riddled windshields and with drivers carrying shotguns. These men were constantly attacked by Eritrean rebels who created roadblocks and then ransacked the vehicles. But they were paid well for their courage. Although we were never attacked, we learned from these men who lived close to the edge. We spent three nights on the road with them. They lived those nights as though they were their last. Every night in the company of different women, and with plenty of *tella*, the local beer. Although they were paid well, we suspected that not much money found its way to the family back home.

———

We talked a lot about Freedom on that journey. In Kristofferson's words: "Just another word for nothing left to lose". Kenya was my home, but it was no longer a hospitable place for white men. Rhodesian whites had declared a Unilateral Declaration of Independence (UDI). South Africa, an horrendous apartheid regime, supported them, but the rest of the world was outraged. Blood was being shed in that beautiful land, a land with many similarities to Kenya. The Tanzanians had swung left, welcoming Chinese and Russian advisers. And many other parts of Africa were already showing signs of instability and hostility toward the outgoing colonial rulers. I was no longer free; I had a lot to lose, starting with my homeland.

On the other hand, if I accepted that my life in Kenya was done, I had nothing left to lose, I was now free to choose anywhere in the world that would let me in. I had no desire to return to the restrictions, the class system, the dreadful, soul-destroying endlessly sunless, dark months that England offered. The rest of Europe seemed scarcely better. But freedom meant more than the ability to find work and settle down. It meant being able to think as I wished, to express my views as I wished, and to do so without the weight of society casting opprobrium upon those choices. Australia beckoned. America sang a siren song.

CHAPTER 12

RIVERS OF BLOOD

1971 – 1973

The Sixties had started with a rash of countries gaining independence. Ten years later these countries were coming to terms with their new freedom, and their new responsibilities. In those countries that had a small white population, the development of this freedom and these responsibilities did not involve racial overtones, or at least not black/white racial overtones. But in others, where the European or Indian population had a significant presence, the racial tension was palpable.

Immediately after Kenya's independence, the British and American governments funded a program, the Million Acre Scheme, to enable African Kenyans to purchase white settler farmland. The alternative – expropriation - was a real possibility, and could have triggered untold violence. This program enabled a peaceful redistribution of the rich and symbolically important White Highlands. Simultaneously, Kenya announced a program to "Africanize" the upper echelons of business and commerce. Work permits were denied to white executives if there was a qualified African applicant. Fortunately this program was administered reasonably in Kenya, and although there was a learning curve, it was not like in the Congo, or even other parts of East Africa. Tanzania moved a little quicker, and in Uganda, once Idi Amin came to power, the pace of Africanization in that country accelerated dramatically.

In 1972, Amin declared all Asians to be personae non gratae in Uganda. Work permits were denied. Businesses were expropriated with risible compensation. More than 80,000 Indians, the backbone of Uganda's commerce, left the country. Some went to Canada, some returned to India, but over 30,000 migrated to England. As always, these refugees were not welcomed. Race relations took on a new dimension in British politics. Enoch Powell, who had spoken so eloquently about Britain's responsibilities in the aftermath of the Hola Massacre rose again to warn against the growing tide of immigrants of color, stating:

"As I look ahead, I am filled with foreboding. Like the Romans,
I seem to see the River Tiber foaming with much blood."

Legislation was passed at the end of the decade restricting the right of entry to Britain by those Citizens of the United Kingdom and Colonies who were not born in Britain and who did not have at least one paternal parent or grandparent born in Britain. This legislation was aimed in large part at the Indian community being ousted from Africa, but I was caught in its net. I did not know it at the time, but discovered its existence some years later when I went to renew my passport as a Citizen of the United Kingdom and Colonies at the British Consulate in Chicago, U.S.A.

After I graduated from University with a Law degree, and passed the Bar exam the next year, my grandfather arranged a position in a well-respected Barristers' chambers in London. While the City was more open than it had been in 1918, the recommendation of a senior judge still carried weight. But I was not ready to settle down, and even less ready to settle into the malaise of England in 1972. I felt stifled.

A series of strikes, by miners, seamen, electricity workers and others, and tax rates as high as 90% on the highest marginal income, led to the collapse of the Labour party. Harold Wilson, the Labour Prime Minister was ousted, and Edward Heath, a Conservative, took his place running the government. The Labour Unions reacted swiftly, calling mass strikes all across the country. England was hobbled, unemployment rose, and worst of all, the country became divided upon class lines. I had no stomach for living in such a country and, in a fateful dinner, told my grandfather that I would not be staying to practice as a Barrister, but that I intended to start a new life either in America (if I could be admitted to the Bar) or in Australia. Barclay's response has stayed with me. He was, of course, deeply disappointed. He hoped that from within the sanctuary of the English Bar, I would be able to achieve some of what eluded him as an outsider. But he did not express this disappointment. Instead, he told me: "I have been a judge for almost fifty years, and although I can decide whether a certain action violated the law, I am aware of my, and Man's, incapacity to judge other men." He recognized that we are all burdened by our past, by our prejudices, by our preferences, and that the act of judging others often speaks volumes more about the judge than about the judged. He wished me God speed, and told me to stay in touch.

Barclay died the next year. I trust that from his resting place he judges that I made a sound decision.

NAIROBI. DECEMBER 1973

Time to say *kwaheri,* good-bye, to Kenya, and to make a life elsewhere. The siren song of America still called. I had contacts there from the safaris in the days of guiding with Tony Church, and the residual sentimental attraction for JFK's "City on a Hill". I had a sense of an American Dream. I was not sure what that dream involved. I believed in a place where neither race, nor class nor money made a difference to one's chances in life; a society that understood that if it "*cannot help the many who are poor, it cannot save the few who are rich.*" I did have these stars in my eyes, but I also believed in the opportunity that America offered to start a new life, one unfettered by background, one in which I could make good money if I worked hard.

Unfortunately, my English law degree meant nothing in America. I would have to go back to Law School and attend the full three years, whereas, with my English degree I could relatively quickly be admitted to practice in Australia or Canada. One of my American friends suggested I take the LSAT[o], and I discovered that it was being offered on Saturday, December 22 at the American Embassy in Nairobi. I decided to take the exam, and if I could be admitted to a good school I would cast my fate with America, otherwise I would head on to Australia. But I could not leave without a special good bye to Lamu.

The week before I left Africa, I persuaded my friends Geraldine and Fiona to join me on a last expedition, a voyage by *jahazi* from Lamu to Malindi. Mohamed Fomu, a ship's captain, had told me that the voyage was only one day to Malindi, and if we left by 5.30 in the morning we were assured of arriving in Malindi by nightfall. And so it was that, at 5.00 o'clock, Wednesday morning, before even the blades of pre-dawn light had cut through the clouds and begun to illuminate the sky, Fi, Gerry and I were scrabbling around in the starlight on the roof of the New Mahrus Hotel in Lamu. The

---

o Law School Aptitude Test, a multiple choice exam which provides an "aptitude" score to Law Schools and is a prerequisite to applying.

sky turned from deep purple to jacaranda to pink. Pink to orange. And finally the sun was up. The Muezzin had long since chanted the *Fajr*, or morning prayer, which ends: *"Assalatu Khayrum minan naum"*, prayer is better than sleep. Men were loading donkeys, and the *ngalawas* were setting sail. Mohamed Fomu was nowhere to be seen. He arrived, regally, after prayers and breakfast, unphased by having kept us waiting, took the helm and ordered the sails unfurled for departure.

The wind in Turkana is hard, and hot, and filled with sand. It stings as it whips your face. It has no mercy, no palliative softness. On Mount Kenya the wind is fickle as a lover. At times a mere whisper, warmed by the sun, it kisses your cheek as you climb. More often, it can turn on you and bite you with its sharp cold teeth. But the wind on the coast, from Dar es Salaam to Malindi and Lamu is gentle, predictable, soothing and kind. The Egyptian cartographer, Ptolemy, who first mapped parts of Africa, said of the East African coast: *"Fair winds, smooth waters and good people mark this land."* The journey from Lamu to Malindi promised to be a gentle journey. The first hours passed with sand dunes to starboard, the ocean to port, and a comfortable breeze on the port transom. Hours slipped by as we lay idly on the deck, gossiping, joking or sleeping. Beaches, mangrove swamps, sand dunes, each drifted by. At one stage, while I was sitting on the bowsprit, a family of porpoises played under me, frolicking in the bow wave. But as the day wore on we did not recognize any signs of habitation, and became concerned that Ptolemy's fair winds had failed us. Which is precisely what happened. Wangavu, the two faced Swahili God of fire and wind decided to look the other way, and as the sun set we were barely half way to Malindi. The sail was furled, fishing lines were cast over the side, and prayer mats appeared on deck for the evening prayer.

There are many kinds of silence. There is the silence after a death, in which the spirit of he who has passed away vibrates the air. There is the silence of a mountain, where the snow and ice crack, the wind cuts through the trees, and a wolf howls. There is the silence of the Sahara in which the stars seem to speak to you, and occasionally, if you are lucky, to laugh with you. I have felt all of these. But that night was filled with the silence of the ocean. Waves lap lightly against the bow, gently rocking the *jahazi*. The wind that has followed us from the Arabian deserts breathes tales of wonder, like those told by Scheherazade. And in those moments of silence there is space to dream. Whose world is so dull that it has no heroes? What child does not dream of great adventure, of fame or glory, of love or passion? I thought of the heroes who filled my youthful years. All Colonials: some of them explorers like Richard Burton, Livingstone and Speke; some of them writers and their heroes, like Rudyard Kipling and Rider Haggard, and even David Crawfurd, hero of John Buchan's tale of adventure, Prester John. Many of them were Kenyans, like Colonel Grogan, Denys Finch Hatton, even George Adamson. Long before Robert Redford portrayed Finch Hatton, his inimical style was legend. He arrived unannounced and left when the wind changed. His pulse beat in the rhythm of Nature, constant yet unpredictable. His love for Karen Blixen was unquestioned, but his comings and goings were as fickle as the wind on Mount Kenya. His courage, his untrammelled sense of opportunity and wildness, his knowledge of the hearts of his bearers, the ways of the animals he hunted, and the spirits that wandered the African night, set him apart. Yet he sat at the feet of Karen Blixen as she wove her tales, and listened to her mesmerized.

As I sat on the *jahazi* that night, sipping tea with Mohamed Fomu, I thought of how this colonial empire had crumbled, its heroes devalued, its leaders shuffled into the historical cobwebs of "men we would rather forget". I wondered about where my road would take me. My family had been Colonials for generations. What would the future hold for its latest tribe of outcasts? Can we cause our mind to dream of visions we wish to harbor? Can we tell it to explore this road or that, to solve the mystery of this puzzle, of that conundrum? Can our mind show us the way forward through our dreams? I asked Mohamed where he wished to be in five years, whether he had plans. His answer was non-committal: "Allah knows all that is in the heavens and on the earth; Allah is Knowing of all things." Clearly he was not a dreamer. Can our dreams have such force that they can make things come true? I thought so then, and think so now. If we dream fervently enough, especially about things that we can control, we can make them come true.

I left Kenya a week later, leaving home and family, leaving the country I loved, the peoples I had grown up with. Destined for continents never visited before. This was my dream and I was excited.

Mohamed Fomu had promised us a trip of one day, arriving Wednesday evening, December 19, but time meant little to this sailor, and we did not arrive at Malindi until the late afternoon of Thursday, December 20, still a full day's bus ride from Nairobi. The Embassy notice informed us to present ourselves for the LSAT Saturday at 8.00 am with a #2 pencil. There were about 10 of us, all Americans except myself, and all much more nervous, much more aware than I, of the importance of the exam. I spent Christmas with the family, and on December 26 stuck out my thumb for rides to South Africa where I planned to find work, save some money and work my passage on a cargo vessel headed for Australia. My relaxed approach to the LSATs served me well, and in early 1974, while selling encyclopedias in Johannesburg, I received news that the scores were good enough to qualify me for many of the better law schools. The decision was made. On to America. I applied to a variety of schools and was accepted at Boston University Law School, starting the fall of 1974.

A client from the Tony Church Safari days put me in touch with a landscape company on Cape Cod, where I worked the summer before school started. I slept on the floor of the attic above the landscape company's garage and worked from 7 to 5 digging ditches, mowing lawns, watering flowers and creating decorative landscapes. Wednesday to Saturday I worked evenings as a wine steward at the Popponesset Inn, an upscale beach club and restaurant for New Yorkers and Bostonians escaping the city. The money was good. With what I saved during that summer, and the next, and a few weekend stints in between, I was able to pay for the first two years of law school. I was fortunate to be accepted at Boston University, but quickly realized that the good jobs out of law school were reserved for those who graduate in the top 10% of the class. So, nose to the grindstone, I applied myself and was rewarded with a job in Chicago in one of the premier law firms in the United States.

CHAPTER 13

AMERICA

"He who dies with the most toys wins"

CABO SAN LUCAS: 1982

"Gentlemen. In 10 minutes we will be landing at the Fonatur airstrip next to your hotel. From the port window you can see the sparkling Sea of Cortez. At this time of year the humpback and blue whales gather here to breed. If you are lucky you might see a school of these wonderful creatures travelling north. From the starboard window, the Sierra de la Garganta mountain range, where Jesuit missionaries built the mission churches of San José de Comondú and San Francisco de Viggé some four hundred years ago. Please fasten your seat belts, tray tables up, seats upright and locked for our descent. We will be landing in a few minutes. You will be met by the hotel car and settled in to the hotel in no time."

The flight attendant did not mention turning off computers and cell phones because, in 1982, they were not yet part of our world. Also, there were only three of us on DK's personal eight-seater Learjet 28. My companions were DK and his investment banking, number-crunching guru, Marco V.

At 32 years old, I was a young lawyer eager to prove my worth and receive the rewards. DK had invited me to spend the week-end on his yacht, moored near Los Cabos, Mexico. We were negotiating the purchase of the historic and beautiful Palmilla hotel, which DK later transformed into one of the iconic resort locations in Baja California. Everything DK touched was successful. After World War II, he started building homes in Newport Beach, and by the 1980s he was rich. Very rich. The two pilots were both ex-military, and the stewardess, whose sole job was to serve drinks and snacks, was young, trim and effusively friendly. That evening, as we stretched out on the lounge chairs of his eighty foot yacht, sipping tequila with a squeeze of fresh limes, DK slapped me on the back and shared one of his pearls of wisdom.

"The secret, Julian, to a happy life, is simply this: He who dies with the most toys wins. And you are with a winner."

I could not find fault with his assessment. What could be better than this? The sun setting behind the hills, the water lapping against the side of the boat. Cabin lights coming on for an exquisite dinner cooked by DK's expert kitchen staff. We did not have to do a thing, lift a finger, other than to summon the waiter, and raise our own glass to our lips. "No doubt about it," I thought, "this is the life. I am going to be a winner, and one day I will have toys. Lots of them. The best toys money can buy."

———

1977 – 2007. THIRTY YEARS A LAWYER

It's easy for Kristofferson to sing about Freedom being just another word for nothing left to lose. But, we have to make a living, feed a family, raise our kids, get them into college, buy a home, pay the medical bills, etc. Reality sets in. And set in it did for me. It was a new drug. The reality drug, which is fueled and condoned by a society that has been high on the drug ever since Consumerism gathered its almost religious zeal. If we all consume more, the economy will grow, and that is good for the country, so it must be good for the individuals who make up the country. This was a very tempting philosophy, and, like Lord Darlington, Oscar Wilde's character in Lady Windermere's Fan, who claimed: "*I can resist anything except temptation*", I did not even attempt to resist.

The early years in a large law firm were then, and still are, hard. But the drug begins to take hold and the long hours feel good. Recognition by one's peers. An excellent starting salary. Training and opportunity. There's a loft development just across the river on the north side of town. Old warehouses being "gentrified" and turned into lofts. Chic new restaurants on the corners. You can walk to work. All young professionals. Cathy, and I purchased a loft with a 90% mortgage. The high monthly payments were not really a problem because we knew that the loft would appreciate (and it did), so working until 8 each night or through Saturday and Sunday of every other weekend did not feel bad. All our friends were doing it, we were all making money. The erosion of personal time, the elimination of space for silence and reflection, these did not matter because we were feeling cool, we were living the American dream. The drug had us hooked.

One thing leads to another, as drugs have a tendency to do. My daughter, Natalie, was born. Cathy returned to work in a few weeks, and I was sequestered in a tax case that took me to Washington D.C. for six weeks within a month of Natalie's birth. We hired Emilia, a lovely Guatemalan lady, to care for our daughter, and we spent an hour of quality time with Natalie when we could get home before her bedtime. When you are an addict you adjust your reality. If it's marijuana you rationalize that all those people who are looking at you strange are indeed Strange themselves. If it's cocaine, you rationalize that you don't need that much sleep, and sure you can function perfectly on four hours sleep, because the coke gives you energy. When you become wedded to a successful career, all the material rewards are your excuse, your justification. We lost our innocence.

Who has the time to watch a sunrise, to drive for days to experience the ancient rituals of the Lost Tribe of Israel, to listen to the chanting of the muezzin at sunset? I forgot about these moments and became absorbed by the toil of making money and the thrill of spending it.

My English roots and identity took a blow when the British Consul in Chicago told me I was not eligible for a British passport. "New law," he said, "all the Asians flooding in from East Africa, driven out by Idi Amin. We had to crack down, and so unfortunately Mr. Nihill, I can only inform you that you are not eligible for British citizenship unless either your father or paternal grandfather was born on British soil." This seemed like the height of insult. "What do you mean," I asked, "No longer British? My citizenship taken away from me just like that. What on earth do you expect me to do? I can't claim American citizenship. Nor am I eligible for Kenyan citizenship. And, no doubt India will not consider me one of its lost sons. Do I look like a potential asylum seeker? I don't think so." I had been a citizen of Great Britain and Colonies for twenty five years. What happened to this identity? Just because Britain had shucked off its colonies, did this now mean I was no longer British? What on earth did it mean to be British, to have been schooled in a British public school and an English University, to have been admitted to the Bar in London? Apparently not much since my father was born in Macao (while his father was in the service of the Queen) and my grandfather was born in Ireland. The Consul finally relented and turned a blind eye. But another blow was struck against my fragile British/colonial identity.

So, I threw myself into the American Dream. For thirty years I lived the life expected of good, hard working American men. Driving hard to succeed. Enjoying the fruits of success. A Porsche. A delightful 1920's stained glass window home. A beautiful wife, and smart, well-adjusted kids. Vacations in exotic places: Myanmar, Botswana, Mallorca, fishing in the Andes. But, I was empty, especially after the children left, because, after all, much of the drive to succeed was fueled by my perception that I had to provide the best for the children. Sure, we were able to afford a first class education, and I have no regrets or second thoughts there. But I do second-guess whether the level of luxury in the travel, the sense that anything was affordable within reason, the opulence of the parties, was good for them.

We had justified the work/life schedule in part by believing that we owed it to our children to provide the best for them. When the children left home the impetus for succeeding financially seemed to fade. As I look back now, I realize that in a strange way these were lost years. The seeds planted in my youth were not fertilized, they did not grow, but remained dormant. The poetry and fascination with humanity that was instilled by Jeannine, was largely suppressed. The commitment to fight for the underdog, the poor and oppressed, learned from grandfather Barclay, simmered below the surface, exhibiting itself in contributions to causes and, for a few years a stint volunteering as a Big Brother in the wonderful Big Brothers, Big Sisters program, but never rose to the level of a driving force in my life. The inquisitiveness and adventurousness imparted by Alan were not explored, for lack of time in a hectic schedule of career and parenting. But, most of all, Nature was forgotten. We spent little time truly immersed in, at one with, the natural world. It was simply easier to view the world from the luxury of the flying carpet that modern travels affords. I regret this loss, especially for my children whose exposure to Nature has been superficial.

We did take many wonderful trips with our children, and as time passed the nature of these trips became a matter of negotiation with Cathy. We both wanted to visit Peru and to see Macchu Picchu. I thought it would be interesting to hike the Inca trail with the children, a walk of about 4 days ending with a climb over a hill and a view from the ridge down onto the mysterious ruins of Macchu Picchu. Cathy wanted to stay at the Monasterio, a beautiful old convent in Cusco, and then take the train to Cusco. We compromised. We stayed at the convent, took the train part way, and walked just one day, the last leg of the Inca Trail.

One of the more interesting, and formative, trips was to Laos and Myanmar, both Buddhist countries. I had become increasingly uncomfortable with Christianity. At one end of the Christianity spectrum, after the death of the great Pope John Paul, Catholicism was undergoing its ice age under Pope Benedict XVI. At the other end, American televangical Christianity was growing stronger and more strident. Islam, too, had taken a shift away from the Islam I knew. Many Muslims in the traditional Muslim heartland from the Middle East to Pakistan had become evangelical and uncompromising. Where was the spirit of acceptance and humanity that

I craved? Hinduism, and the exotic spirituality of India never appealed to me. My logical lawyer brain found it to be much hocus-pocus. But I was intrigued by the peacefulness of the Dalai Lama who I had heard speak in Colorado. I liked the idea of a religion in which Man's connection with his maker was more direct, and less subject to man-made rules of behavior.

Laos is a deeply religious Buddhist country. Most young men spend time in a monastery (much as I did in my youth). They follow complex and rigid rules of behavior, including rising before dawn, not eating after the midday meal, extensive meditation and rituals. The monks survive primarily on the largesse and generosity of the population, and one of the more beautiful rituals is the daily pre-dawn procession of monks through Luang Prabang, during which the local population gives food, most typically rice, to the monks. While we were all moved by the sincere appreciation the people have for the monks, and by the respect shown them, we were saddened by the tourists who jumped in front of the monks and snapped flash photographs. We wondered how people could come to such a spiritual place and behave with so little spirituality. We talked with some monks about the core values of the monastery: Humility, unselfishness, discipline and compassion, and wondered how our world would be different if we focused an hour or so a day meditating on these attributes and on how we could nurture these values within ourselves. But the French had ruled Laos for many years, and even with the sincere beliefs of the devout Buddhists, we perceived a certain laissez faire attitude to life that we attributed to the French colonization. I was eager to move on to Myanmar.

Myanmar, formerly Burma, seems feudal, even by Southeast Asian standards. Outside of the capital, Rangoon (or Yangon), the country is poor and rural. The main tourist attractions are Inle Lake and Bagan, where the early Bamar kings held court and built over 2000 temples and stupas. The main attraction of Inle Lake is its population of fishermen who have developed a unique style of rowing, grasping the oar, or extended paddle, with their toes while they stand and look out over the weeds and plants that would otherwise obstruct their view. It is a peaceful world, uncluttered and simple. But, for us the most interesting day involved a hike to a rural market, one of many that occur on a rotating basis during the year. The setting could have jumped out of the scenes of Belgian peasant life in feudal Europe by Pieter Breughel. Ox carts; pigs being dragged to market on a decaying rope; chickens in coops made from strands of dried weeds hanging from the shoulder of an ancient horse; barter and more barter, nearly all transactions being conducted without the exchange of money. And all of this occurring while the Bamar lords of Myanmar drove Mercedes in Yangon and sent their children to schools in Switzerland.

———◆———

In Walden, Henry David Thoreau asks:

"How many a man has dated a new era in his life from the reading of a book. The book exists for us perchance which will explain our miracles and reveal new ones."

After the children left home, I found myself reading Thoreau, Whitman, Saint-Exupéry and others, of whom more later. I have no doubt that these books marked a "new era" in my life, but they were sowing seeds on fertile ground. What was it that made the ground fertile? What led me to be receptive to their views?

I cannot point to any single, cathartic moment, but I am conscious of a gradual sense of alienation from the prevailing zeitgeist of our time. Like aging, one day you realize that while you enjoy bike riding, it is no longer fun to ride in a pack that is timing the laps around the lake; or you discover that you do not understand what your children are talking about when they are discussing music or technology. In the '60s, and even in the early '70s when I arrived in Boston, I was among a majority who shared Kennedy's commitment to a society in which those with privilege felt a responsibility to others less fortunate. By 1980, within a few years of my graduating from Law School, his call for a society that will "help the many who are poor" no longer resonated, neither for me nor for much of American society. Without thinking about it, I became part of what Aaron Barlow has called "The Cult of Individualism", an admiration, a quasi-deification, of the man (or woman) who has pulled himself up by his bootstraps to realize financial success, or who has redefined himself to create a new, successful persona. In the biography section of my library today, Anchee Min (a powerful advocate of Individualism, and author of two autobiographies, *Red Azalea* and *Cooked Seed)* rests by Menchu, Maathai and Mandela; Bill Gates is next to Guevara; and Jobs and Lyndon Johnson are on the same shelf as Kahlo and King. I have no doubt that this Individualism has been integral to the success of our capitalist, consumerist culture. But, gradually, as I had more time to reflect, it made me uncomfortable. I thought of the settlers in the White Highlands of Kenya, how they, and many other white Kenyans honestly believed not only that it was their innovation, their vision, their toil, that had made Kenya the idyllic place they knew it to be, but they also believed that if left to the Africans, the country would go to the dogs. Few were interested in seeing the Africans educated, in finding meaningful jobs, or in participating in the process of government. The prevailing sense was highly tribal: Our White tribe against your Black tribe. But more egregious, more insidious, was the sense, almost the mantra, that it was not their responsibility to assist the Africans to realize their potential. While the overtly religious overtone of the prior century was no longer prevalent, the era in which British Empire advocates openly expressed the idea that God had created the White Man as a superior race, the fact remained that many whites, including those in government, felt that it was the African's fault that he was still in abject poverty, and that it was through the white man's (individual and collective) efforts that he was the ruler. The Cult of Individualism that prevails in America today smacks of the same prejudice.

I did not then, and I do not now, criticize the Capitalist/ Consumer culture. It succeeds dramatically at achieving precisely what it is designed to achieve, i.e. spurring invention, reducing cost, increasing profit. But, it was not working for me. I had a deep-seated feeling that we were overlooking the concomitant responsibility for others that comes with success and with privilege. While I was no longer a practising Catholic, the ghosts of sermons past tugged at my conscience. By the time I turned 50, I was beginning to feel that the men I had admired – Kennedy; Nyerere; Grandfather Barclay; Abbot Basil Hume – were slipping away from me. I was like a caterpillar, plodding, consuming voraciously, storing up wealth for what … a voyage, a metamorphosis whose form and outcome I could not conceive.

CHAPTER 14

OUTWARD BOUND IN MEXICO

2006

Over one hundred years ago, Henry David Thoreau struggled with the question of the meaning of life. He built a small shack in the woods of New Hampshire, and spent two years there, absorbing the pace of nature, learning what life had to teach. Why did he choose this route? Thoreau writes:

> *I went to the woods because I wished to live deliberately, to front[p] only the essential facts of life, and see if I could not learn what it had to teach, and not, when I came to die, discover that I had not lived.*

As I read Walden, Thoreau's description of these two years, I thought: When I "come to die" will I discover that I have not lived? How will I measure whether I have indeed lived? What does it mean, to have "lived"? Clearly, merely existing on the planet's surface is not Living. For some, Living might be counting the number of parties they attended, the times they got drunk with friends and sang, the times they met a new girl. For others it might be the sunrises or sunsets experienced. Yet others might count the houses, the

___
p Confront

cars, the travels, the museums, the books, the movies, and so on. I realized that for me, Living has been finding awe in the magnificence of the mountains, finding peace in the motion of the ocean's waves, and finding common ground and spirit with the animals, and birds, and fish of the wilderness.

Thomas Arnold, Headmaster of the prominent English boys boarding school, Rugby, advised his pupils, more than 150 years ago, that "Life is not a Having and a Getting, but a Being and Becoming." If that is the case, What should we Be and who should we Become?

Thoreau's challenge, Arnold's exhortation, and the sensation of disconnectedness that I was beginning to feel, troubled me as I entered my fifties. The children had left for college, embarked on their own lives. Cathy and I were on our own. We had a lot of space, both physical space in the house, and temporal space in our days, to fill. Thus began a rediscovery of paths untrodden and overgrown, of seeds that had hibernated long enough, of a world of the senses somewhat forgotten.

The Trustees of my children's high school, an excellent academic institution in Dallas, had embarked on the preparation of a 10 year Strategic Plan. I was honored to be chosen to chair the Education Committee. Our first task was to define the goals and values that would drive our 10-year plan. This is more difficult than it seems at first. It is easy to mouth the platitudes of Honor, Respect, Diligence, etc. But, very quickly the conversation turns to academic results, how many students are admitted to top tier Universities. And one has to wonder what is important in education. This exercise led me to believe, strongly, that academics should be secondary to inquisitiveness, adventurousness and awareness for the rights of others.

During the summer of 2004, while negotiating a joint venture for the operation of a dive recompression chamber in Zanzibar, I met Francois Burman, the Chairman of Outward Bound in South Africa. I knew of Outward Bound from my childhood, and was eager to learn how it had evolved, how it was doing in South Africa. Francois invited me to spend a week at the Outward Bound School. I accepted without hesitation and was delighted to see a school that was breaking racial barriers, developing self esteem and compassion in a society wracked by decades of segregation and hatred.

That experience lead me, in turn, to found the Outward Bound School in Mexico, where we are dedicated to helping young people develop their self esteem, their tenacity, their commitment to the environment and to humanity, and finally, their integrity and compassion. In its essence, Outward Bound is about challenging people to leave their comfort zone and to grow as they learn to cope with the unfamiliar, the frightening, and the difficult. In 1940, when Outward Bound was founded by Kurt Hahn this was a new way of thinking. Today, even authors of self-help books use the same methodology. Our focus was on Youth At Risk.

In November 2010 I received a call from Claudia Navarro, the head of a group within the Mexico City government called the CEAA, the Comunidad Externa de Atención para Adolescentes.

"Julian, we need OB to do a program for us as soon as possible."

"We are booked for the next couple of weeks. Why the hurry?"

"We have budget this year, but as of December 1 we start a new budget year, and the funds we have today are gone if we don't spend them."

"OK, tell me a little about the profile of the youth you wish to send on an OB Expedition with us."

"There are some 3,000 youth between ages 15 and 18 incarcerated in the City of Mexico. About 2,500 are males in the prison at X. Some 350 are women in the prison at Y. Another 80 are in an institution for mentally disturbed, and the remaining 70 or so are in a prison at Z. We want to send 10 or 12 youth from this last group."

"And the profile of this last group? Who are they?"

"Ah, they have all committed homicide. They are in the last month of their sentence and we want to do all we can to prevent them from falling back into the criminal culture."

At which point Patrick, our Program Director, interjects despondently "Great, Outward Bound's first assassins' program."

We ran the program two weeks later. Patrick and two of our tougher instructors led a group of twelve. One prison psychologist joined the group. On the first day one youth collapsed. He had obtained some drugs en route from prison to the beginning of the program and was simply unable to function. The next day one participant ran away. He was found six hours later at his mother's house. The remaining ten plugged on. It was a six-day expedition from Valle de Bravo (at 5,000 feet) to the peak of the Nevado de Toluca (15,500 feet). On the third day the group hit the classic storming moment. The leader of the storming was a heavily tattooed, older youth, who was clearly a leader within the jail hierarchy. The storming turned into a revolt. The other participants were afraid to express themselves against the wishes of the leader, and our instructor team feared a complete collapse.

Fortunately, Cesar, one of the instructors, had spent several years within the prison in Cancun working with an alternative art program. His language was as tough as that of any Mexico City gang youth, and his experience with hardened criminals even more profound. Catch

Cesar in the right mood, and he will keep you on the edge of your chair for hours with tales of the drug lords in prison, how they had suites within the jail, their own structure of power and abuse, and, most entertainingly, monthly parties with alcohol, drugs and girls from the street. All under the umbrella of a corrupt prison system.

Cesar took control, and gradually the group came back into shape. The seeds of Performing were sown. The group stayed together, and although the group leader declined the attempt to summit the peak on the sixth day, seven of the youth made it to the top. The result was a huge boost in self-esteem for the successful group, and a sense of remorse and failure in the one who ran away and in the leader who opted out on the last day. It was clear to the instructors that he was afraid to fail, and rather than subject himself to that failure he checked out, but when the others returned successful, he lost status.

Claudia called a month later:

"We have reviewed all the programs that we have tried this year, and almost unanimously the psychologists have evaluated the OB program as the most powerful. So, the good news is that we have obtained a budget for six more programs in 2011."

Obviously I was delighted at her assessment. In May 2011, I attended the graduation, about two weeks after the expedition ended, of the participants in a 21-day program. Even I was amazed. Mothers and fathers weeping at the change in their child. How respectful he or she was. How much he/she wanted to forego drugs and the street, and how some of them had already found jobs. And the youth, to a person, thanking us for the change we had effected.

I was sure then that dying with the most toys was not the goal. Dying with experiences such as this was clearly more rewarding.

CHAPTER 15

KILIMANJARO AND SOKOKE

2009 & 2010

"Hey, Dad, you're slowing down. We need to nail some challenging adventures before you slide into senility."

I bristled, piqued by Barclay's unspoken challenge. Cheeky lad. "What's that supposed to mean?" I replied.

"You're celebrating your 60th in a couple of months. AARP card in the mail. Discounts on the subway. Advertisements featuring old guys throwing footballs through tires. Why don't we celebrate your impending old age by climbing Kili together?"

More precisely, his suggestion was that we should climb Kilimanjaro, all 19,341 feet of it, that Christmas holidays. His challenge triggered memories of the time, almost forty years earlier, when Dave Harries and I had climbed Mount Kenya, how we looked across the plains of Africa toward Kilimanjaro some two hundred miles away, and promised ourselves: that would be our next expedition. We never made that climb. I sensed that some unfinished business could be closed with this expedition. Barclay and I agreed: the two of us would summit together on Christmas morning, 2009.

Little did I know, when I accepted the challenge, that this return to East Africa would trigger a string of sensations, memories, and realizations that would lead to profound changes in my life.

The first night on the mountain, as we lay beside the camp fire, the evening still warm, the sounds of plains game in the distance, my mind drifted back to exploring Kenya with Dave Harries, to the dhow trip from Lamu to Mombasa, to the host of memories of East Africa. I grew to love the land and call it my own. But, in 1973 I had chosen to leave, to pursue a yearning to grow as an individual and to become more than the aggregate of my past experiences. Now I had returned, and in the next five days not only would I experience the journey up Kilimanjaro and back, but I would reflect on what had caused me to leave Africa, and what brought me back. As the saying goes: *You can take the boy out of Africa, but you can't take Africa out of the boy.*

Kilimanjaro is the tallest mountain in Africa. It bursts out of the plains of the Serengeti, like a coffee cake covered with sweet white frosting, an enormous volcano, its caldera stretching 2.5 kilometers across. There are many approaches to and routes up the mountain. We chose the Rongai route from the north because few people come this way and its approach is relatively gentle. Although Kilimanjaro is surrounded by game parks, including Serengeti, Amboseli, and uncle Max's beautiful jewel, Manyara National Park, there is currently very little large animal life in its foothills. Man has won that battle for territory. Today the northern foothills of Kilimanjaro are populated by Chagga tribes-people, an industrious, agricultural people. Wildness and wilderness have receded.

Approaching the entrance to Kilimanjaro National Park, we drove past groups of women, wrapped in colorful *kikois*, carrying stacks of vegetation longer than themselves, perched on their heads. Others carried sticks for the evening fire, tied in bundles resting on their backs and hanging by a leather strap from their foreheads.

The trail meanders through fields of high maize plants and shorter rows of tomatoes strung along low suspender posts. As evening falls we see two women with large pestles pounding corn in a wooden mortar. They face each other, and as one pounds, the other raises her pestle in the air, momentarily letting go as the pestle rises in the air, and claps her hands above her head. They sing as they work, happy in their simple world.

Our first morning on the mountain dawns clear and bright. Today we walk some 7 hours, ascending gradually. It is not strenuous. We start in pine forest where we see Colobus monkeys, spotting them through the trees by the flash of their long white tails. They are gregarious and inquisitive, not prone to hide from sight. We catch glimpses of the Blue Monkeys, which are no more Blue than the Blue Men Tuaregs. Their bodies are a dark slate, their faces a lighter grey, and the front of their throats a dirty white. Above about 9,000 feet plant life struggles and forest gives way to moorland. There are few animals once you reach this level, apart from mice and other small rodents. There are raptors, augur buzzards whose white chests and white underside wings tipped with black make a fabulous sight against a clear blue sky. But most beautiful, especially on a bright morning, is the scarlet tufted malachite sunbird, whose brilliant green head and long curved beak are reminiscent of a hummingbird. These splendid birds are plentiful, sucking nectar from the giant lobelias that sprout randomly across the moor.

After a fine breakfast of eggs, bacon and sausage, the porters pack up camp and we climb unburdened. The hard work is all being done by the porters who carry not just sleeping bags, tents and food, but the mess tent, the cooking supplies and all our gear. I walk beside my son, and think of James Joyce's description of himself in *Portrait of an Artist as a Young Man*:

> *"He was alone. He was unheeded, happy, and near to the wild heart of life. He was alone and young and wilful and wildhearted, alone amid a waste of wild air and brackish waters and the seaharvest of shells and tangle and veiled grey sunlight."*

Barclay and I shared that sense of unheededness with Joyce, with Stephen Dedalus and with each other. The adventure lay ahead.

But I also felt ill at ease with the luxury of the hike. For as long as we had lived in America, we had carried our own food, our tents, our supplies, when we camped. This pampering was uncomfortable for me. I was unaccustomed to it. I offered to help Mwangari as he loaded yet another duffle bag into the enormous pile he was carrying, and was rebuffed. Walking up the mountain, I fell in with Peter, our lead guide. He was a man about my age, a Chagga, born here in the foothills. He had not known another life. He was educated in a rural school run by Catholic priests and had learned a few words of English, but never had the chance to use them until, at 15, he started as a porter and graduated to being a guide. Now his English was good, his sense of protocol with clients well honed, even a certain European sense of humour. I asked him if he knew Lake Manyara, the nearby park. Of course he did, he said. I told him about my uncle Max, the first warden of the park. He did not know Max, but he had heard of him, of how he resembled a plover running along the shore of the lake with his long skinny legs and his beaky face. We chatted and reminisced, but it was an awkward reminiscence because now our roles had changed. He was leading and I was following. Fifty years earlier he could not have approached me freely; he would have had to wait for me to say Hello. I probably would not have noticed him. I, a white colonial child, in his country, his African country, which my people had adopted as their own. Peter could have been one of those wide eyed little boys who stood timidly behind the walls of their huts where their parents lived, houseboys, cooks, gardeners, drivers, all dependent on the whims of their colonial masters. Now we walked together. He smoked and told tales of earlier ascents, of clients whose behaviour seemed to me to beg belief, but to him was simply part of the European's way of being. We spoke some Swahili together, bringing us closer, linked in our common humanity, but still oceans apart.

My prevailing memory of the first three days is one of dampness. It either rained or sleeted every day until we reached Mawenzi, the peak that marks the beginning of the slog up to the Kibo camp, the last refuge before the ascent on the summit. Our clothes were wet. The tents and even the sleeping bags had a damp mustiness because the sun remained swaddled in clouds thoughout those first three days. For much of the time we could not see Kili or Mawenzi up ahead. The mist had fallen low on the mountain, obscuring all that was below and behind us. On a shoulder close to Mawenzi there lies the wreckage of a six-seater Cessna 206 that crashed in November 2008, killing its four Italian tourist passengers. Its fuselage, like the body of a beheaded grasshopper, intact some fifty feet from the cockpit. The wings torn and shattered, strewn across the barren landscape. No one has ventured to clean up the wreckage. Africa leaves its detritus where it dies.

The ascent on the summit started a little before midnight that Christmas eve. We had hiked for four days: through the thickly vegetated foothills of Kilimanjaro, alive with birdsong, and the chattering of monkeys; across the moonlike, foggy, arid stretches above the tree line, damp and cold, day and night; to the camp by the beautiful blue green tarn at the base of Mawenzi Peak, splendidly steep and imposing, where we slept for the last time; and on to the Kibo huts at 15,500 feet where we rested for an afternoon and evening before beginning our ascent.

On this last leg, we climbed for about six hours and some 3,800 feet from the high camp at the Kibo Huts. A sprinkle of snow covered our early steps, but by 2.00 a.m. we heard the crunch of deeper snow with every step we took. The silence was broken by the wind, the crunching of our footsteps in the crisp new snow, and the sound of our breathing, heavier with each step as the air became thin. The blackness of the sky, the brilliance of the stars, and the eerie reflection of a soft light on the snow enveloped us. As we looked behind we saw twinkling lines of lights, the headlamps of other groups of climbers, snaking upward like pilgrims. Then the guides began to sing. First a hum, a murmur, a familiar tune, but one we could not yet place. The words made no sense. Suddenly we realized: Christmas carols, songs we had sung as children, but in Kiswahili. The guides in the group behind us took up the refrain. In the African tradition of call and response, one group sang a verse and the next replied with a chorus, another verse, a hum or a repetition. At that moment, the stars and the blackness, the silence and the crunching, the cold air and our warm breaths, joined in an eternity that linked us more closely to the first Christmas night than I have ever been before or since.

Around 3.00 a.m. our group was struggling with the altitude and falling behind the goal of reaching the rim of Kilimanjaro's crater by sunrise. One of the guides suggested that Barclay and I and a young couple from Iceland break off and move ahead.

We reached Gilman's Point, on the rim of the crater shortly before sunrise that Christmas morning. The night was so clear, the stars so many and so bright, the reflection off the snow so vivid in the blackness, that we could trace the ridgeline to the summit. As we looked East, the faintest tinge of orange appeared above the miles and miles of fluffy white clouds, thick as cotton wool, resting on the plains of Africa. To the West the great glacier formation loomed. They said the glacier was shrinking, a victim of global warming, but this cold, Christmas morning, the glacier walls loomed large and eternal, reflecting the first rays of sunlight with a soft blue tone.

Barclay stepped away to sit alone, to contemplate the vastness stretched out before us, without another soul in sight. I had left East Africa almost forty years earlier, convinced it was no place for a young white man starting his career. Even then my heart ached with a kind of homesickness for this land, these eternal skies, this serene solitude. But at the same time it was filled with excitement and anticipation for the new world I was to visit, the new life I was about to create. What had gone wrong? Why was I back here, feeling that same homesickness again, decades later?

Barclay's voice broke the spell. "Damn it, Dad. It's crazy. This side is Kenya, and that side is Tanzania, all because some fat Queen, sitting in her palace in London, decided to make a gift to her poor grandson who did not have a mountain in Africa. What on earth did she know about the people who live here, and what right did she have to decide which country they should belong to. It's all so random."

There are natural boundaries on the earth's surface, oceans and rivers, mountains, creeks and forests. Other boundaries are drawn by Man, often as quixotically as the dent in the line between Kenya and Tanzania. Some of these lines separate man from man, tribe from tribe, even race from race. But from the top of Africa's highest mountain no such boundaries appear. The plains of East Africa stretch far and wide across Tanzania and Kenya, from the Indian Ocean to the lakes that run down the Rift Valley, this valley that is the cradle of mankind, this rift that runs through Ethiopia and Kenya, through Tanzania and on into Mozambique. That is a natural boundary, but it has nothing to do with Nations. Our ancestors, Zinjanthropus and "Lucy", travelled the length of this Rift, hunting, finding shelter, raising their young. From Olduvai to Turkana, and on to the Afar Delta, in the shadow of Mount Kenya and Kilimanjaro, through the White Highlands and the Chalbi desert, this was their land.

Today it is home to the Serengeti, teeming with wild game, the land of the Great Migration. I was so familiar with the rhythm of the savannahs of East Africa that the image of what was happening below those clouds was clear to me. A young wildebeest was shaking off the night. Awakened by the call of a flock of yellow-necked spur fowl and the cooing of ring neck doves, he was groggily rising to his feet. Front legs bent like an acolyte in prayer, hind legs and rump in the air, he unsteadily extended his matchstick front legs until he was standing. With a frisky whisk of his tail, and a shake of his mane, he trotted over to his mother. The bright weaverbirds chirped, the yellow-throated long claw sang a morning welcome, and the day began. Not a mile away, a large, black-maned, male lion, rolled over from his torpid slumber onto his belly. Shook his massive head and looked into the distance toward the rising sun. His day and that of the young wildebeest would start apart and end together.

These creatures know no boundaries, and nor do I. I have no home, no roots, no soil to call my own. No nation claims my allegiance, nor will I assert my right, or that of my tribe, to populate any segment of our planet. Today, alas, tribal bonds still bind the men of Africa to fight one against the other. Hutu and Tutsi, Kikuyu and Luo, Hausa and Yoruba. Religions stir men to fight and kill each other over the pettiest differences: Protestant and Catholic in Northern Ireland; Sunni and Shia in Iraq; even in America, the land of the free, the melting pot of the world, new tribal allegiances are being formed, stoked by leaders and demagogues whose power increases as tribal animosity intensifies. A dangerous trend. Tribal attitudes nearly destroyed the land of my birth, and I have no place for them.

Sitting on the rim of Kilimanjaro, looking over the sea of clouds, I thought of how peoples through time immemorial have housed their Gods in mountains. Mount Olympus, home to the Gods of the Greeks. Mount Kailash in Tibet, sacred to Buddhists and Hindus alike. Everest, home of Miyolangsangma, the Goddess of Inexhaustible Giving. And Mount Kenya, home to Ngai, the God of the Kikuyu. Who and where were my Gods? From early childhood numerous Gods had populated my planetarium. Hindu Gods, Greek Gods, the Buddha and, of course, the Christian God, whose monks trained my thinking. But that day, other Gods spoke to me. The God of the wind stroked and chilled my cheeks.

The God of the morning light danced gracefully to the East. The God that brought peoples from Africa and Asia, from Europe and America to stand on this peak together that Christmas day, a God of inclusion, a God of love, infused my soul. The God that created me as just another animal, but one whose species was privileged to be able to look beyond family and tribe, to reach out to others with compassion and humanity. This was my God.

The ascent from Gilman's Point to the summit is gentle and, apart from the altitude, is not difficult. As you walk south along the rim of the volcano, the wall of the broad, snow filled crater drops to your right. Ahead of you and to your left, is the glacier, a towering wall of snow and ice. The early morning sun strikes the glacier and casts a blue tinge to the clear ice formations. The air has a thinness that makes breathing a challenge, and hampers your progress, but it also feels light, and pure. We reached the summit in less than an hour. Others were there ahead of us. There was a festive feeling. A couple, a tall, slim African man and his athletic American bride, had just been pronounced Man and Wife. They were both dressed in white. He, in a white suit and red top hat; she in a soft white dress over warm white thermal underwear. Barclay and I shared their moment and then turned to our own reflections about the meaning of this moment.

———

Before I headed back to Mexico I saw the chess set Jeannine had had made for me in Bagamoyo fifty years earlier. I asked if I could take it with me back to Mexico.

"You know how it is Mum," I told her, "sometimes you don't realize how much you miss something until you see it again, and then a stream of memories come back to you. Dad and I played on this chess set many an evening. He taught me about castling, about the Ruy Lopez opening, and the Sicilian Defense, about taking a pawn *en passant,* and about flooding the board with attacking pieces. But not just that, I remember holding the pieces and turning them over in my hands, admiring the elephant's delicate tusks and the dynamism of the drumming pawns. How did you get them to create these pieces?"

"Oh, just trial and error. Old Juma was a quick learner and once he understood that I was not looking for something that looked like it was destined for a curio shop on Jamhuri Street, but that we should recreate African village life, he was a great partner in the design."

"I have missed these things. May I take it with me?" I asked.

"Of course, darling, and may you enjoy playing with it now as much as you did as a boy."

———

When Angelica visited my apartment for the first time about a year later, some weeks after our stroll down Horacio and the snatch of verse from Verlaine, one of the first things that caught her eye was the chess set. Before the photographs of the Rendille girls, before the djembes resting beside the Lamu bed and my collection of East African musical instruments, before the Maasai shield and the Makonde carvings. She was fascinated by the design, the syncretism of the African and European styles, the weaving of an African lifestyle into an ancient Persian game. I told her the story of its creation, of my mother's affection for Bagamoyo and the old woodcarvers. Of sitting in the shade of an ample girthed baobab tree, mesmerized by the bao board as the baobab seeds were shuffled from hole to hole.

"Did you ever read Howard's End?" she asked.

"Of course, D.H. Lawrence. It was required reading in High School."

"*No fue* Lawrence, *tonto*. *Fue* E. M Forster." Switching to English: "Sometimes you are too big for your shoes."

"Or maybe even my boots."

"*Zapatos, botas, cualquier.* One of the themes of the book is the need to connect. "*Only connect the prose and the passion, and both will be exalted.*" I feel that there is a passion for Africa within you that you don't permit to connect to your life today. And I suspect that by ignoring it, you do not let it, or your present life, be exalted."

"Maybe. May well be."

As I turned the chess pieces over in my hand, caressing the smooth back of the knight/elephant, rubbing the serrated edge of the thatched hut/castle, I remembered the old men, the children running to the beach, the chickens pecking at worms, and the baobab tree. Baobabs are huge and fat and ugly. Their branches barely bloom. Instead, they look like they were planted upside down, their heads in the ground, searching for their roots.

And I missed Africa. That was before I invited her to Kenya, before I saw Africa again through her eyes.

———————

Returning from Kilimanjaro to live alone in Mexico I had a lot of time to reflect on the time on Kilimanjaro: The connection with

Nature, the relationship with the peoples of Kenya, the themes of wealth and personal fulfillment. I thought about the difference between my trip to the Sea of Cortez with Angelica, and the trip thirty years earlier with DK. With DK I had been in the lap of luxury; with Angelica we were in a most simple sailboat. The luxury, the presence of Man and his trappings, the pampering by attentive flunkies, did not enhance the moment; they got in the way. If a whale shark had swum under DK's yacht, much less a pair of dolphins, we would not have known. Was Hahn correct when he suggested that *"wealth, power and a sense of entitlement"* were chains from which we must be set free? Was Thoreau on the right track when he decided to *"go to the woods to live deliberately"*? What about men like Paul Farmer and Greg Mortensen, were they really happier living a life without possessions? I re-read Saint-Exupery's *The Little Prince*. Toward the end of the book, the Little Prince is consoling his human friend because he is going to return to his star, Asteroid B-612. He tells his friend that *"people have stars, but they aren't the same."* For most people, he says, their stars are "silent stars", but, he tells his friend, *"You'll have stars that laugh."* I wish for stars that laugh, for the pace of a day walking with the nomads and their camels in the desert, for the miles of open plains watching wildebeest and giraffe and impalas graze, for the simple pleasure of trading toothpaste for copper bracelets with a Rendille girl girding her camel for a house moving, for the rattle of the stays against the mast, and for the sensation of dolphins swimming by or elephants grazing behind the tent. All of these I had known, but in recent years I had forgotten. As I grew closer to Angelica, and started to see the world through her eyes, I thought: Was my *langeur* born of this absence?

When Angelica and I visited Kenya in 2010 we visited the Sokoke Forest on the coast between Mombasa and Malindi. It is essentially an isolated forest of tall trees and thick bushes. It is home to the shy and fascinating elephant shrew, which is neither elephant nor shrew, but whose orange color and peculiar proboscis inspire images of animals now extinct and found only in children's coloring books. Sokoke is populated with large colonies of vervet monkeys whose varying alarm calls can be heard across vast expanses of forest, announcing the presence, in differentiated tones, of leopard, eagles or pythons. But, the forest's primary attraction is its amazing bird life. The Clarke's Weaver is completely endemic to the forest, while the Sokoke Scops Owl, Sokoke Pipit, and the Amani Sunbird are found only in one other coastal park, in Tanzania. There are birds hidden everywhere in the thick forest. Vereaux's Eagle owls hoot sonorously, Paradise flycatchers twitter, a variety of doves coo, and brown-headed parrots screech. Angelica and I walked this forest with our bird-guide, Jonathon. He would imitate these birdcalls and elicit a response. Often, the response was followed by the appearance of the bird responding to the call. As evening approached, Jonathon bade us farewell and suggested we drive to a spot near the edge of the park where, with luck, we might witness the pilgrimage of a small herd of elephants to a watering hole in the woods.

All animals have their own beauty, but for sheer majesty there is nothing to compare with a herd of elephants. We parked our Land Rover in a dense clump of trees down wind of the watering hole so that we would not be conspicuous. And waited. The forest was behind us; an open meadow, no bigger than a couple of football fields, lay in front of us. In the middle of the meadow was a muddy pond some forty feet wide. The setting sun painted the western sky a deep red, shot through with streaks of orange. As darkness began to fall, and the red turned to purple, there was an explosion of sound. Crickets rubbing their wings frantically set up a constant hum, the vibrato of the violin section of the orchestra. The eagle owls and trumpeter hornbills sung loud their tunes, the clarinets and flutes of the performance. Frogs, fat on their haunches, eyes bulbous, their throats pulsating, let out deep, powerful croaks, the base notes of the evening.

At that moment a large matriarch elephant appeared from the forest to our left and behind us. She walked slowly, apparently alone. Her trunk was up, testing the wind, swinging left and right, up and around, smelling for humans or other dangers. In her youth, in the 1970's, it is probable that she had been hunted, that she had seen the decimation caused by poachers, and she was still leery of human contact. Her large ears flapped, possibly enabling her to listen better. She lifted her right foot and held it there, in the air, balanced for a moment between retreating and progressing. On a signal from the matriarch, the rest of the herd began to emerge. First a couple of mid aged males, neither of them large or old enough to challenge the matriarch for leadership, but both in line and competing for rank. Then some females, some with little calves struggling to stay within the protection of their mothers. They advanced slowly, a herd of about eighteen, to the water. They did not all drink at once. The older elephants took turns in staying on guard, watching and listening for danger. The younger ones frolicked, rolled in the muddy water, sprayed each other and hid behind their mothers. They remained for about ten minutes, and then the matriarch raised her trunk again, let out a soft trumpet sound, and started to walk back to the forest on our right. The herd followed except for two very young elephants that lingered, playing in the water. A young adult, noticing their absence, trotted back, and tucking his tusks under their rumps, cajoled them into joining the herd.

Ten years earlier this herd was under extraordinary pressure. Poachers had decimated a large part of the elephant population of the coastal area of Kenya, and this herd, like many others, had to live secluded in the forest, rarely venturing out to this watering hole, and only in the very driest season. This evening, however, as they did night after night, the local children had gathered in the distance to witness the majesty of the herd, to be transported into a world in which these gigantic creatures frolic like children. These young Kenyans are growing up treasuring their natural heritage, and they will fight to keep the forest in place, even when a Chinese hotel chain offers to build a five star resort here and to cure all the illnesses of all the children in their family. They will know that if we win the battle against Nature we will realize we were on the wrong side.

CHAPTER 16

SAHARA: THE INWARD JOURNEY

2014

Life is serendipitous. We can plan to be somewhere, to do something, to share an experience with someone, and often that plan will be fulfilled. But, often, too, if we just let the plan take care of itself we find ourselves lifted by the winds of fate and transported to a distant place, a remote experience, like the seeds of maple trees with their helicopter wings that carry them miles from where they would have fallen if their trajectory had been straight downward. Two years earlier I had set the seed of this trip with my friend from Kenya, Michael Asher, the world's leading expert on the Sahara. He had invited me to walk the route Lord Kitchener took across Northern Sudan to rescue Gordon from the Mahdi in Khartoum. That trip had been cancelled because of the war in Sudan, so Christmas 2012, sitting in front of an atlas in Michael's drawing room nestled into the Langata forest where leopards roam and giraffe slope across his lawn, we traced our fingers across the Sahara.

"None of the Northern tier of countries is worth visiting if you want the real Sahara," Michael said, "Morocco, Algeria, Tunisia, Libya, Egypt. Either overrun by tourists in Land Rovers, like the luxury three day camping trips into the Erg Chebbi desert and on to Merzouga and Ourzazate, or overrun by Al Qaeda."

"I rather fancied the Morocco trip myself. I remember a lovely book by Sylvia Kennedy called *See Ourzazate and die*. Can't we start there, in Ourzazate, and just go deeper than the Land Rovers?"

"Not really. Its all become bloody commercial. Even the Tuareg have become commercial, and you can't find peace, or solitude, much less an authentic Saharan expedition. It's a show, not a cultural immersion."

"OK, what about the next tier of countries?" I asked, tracing my finger across Northern Africa. "Mauritania, Mali, Niger..."

"Mauritania really has the most beautiful dunes and landscapes in all the Sahara," Michael commented, "but it is impossibly unsafe now. Completely in the thrall of Al Qaeda."

"And Mali? I have always wanted to go to Mali. They have fantastic music there, and a great music festival in Bamako. Remember *Dimanche in Bamako*, the album by Amadou and Mariam. And Ali Farka Touré. He's from Mali, isn't he?"

"Sure. Actually, the Desert Festival was held outside of Timbuktu, not Bamako, and the radical Muslim influence has banned the event starting next year. Mali is really not safe for westerners, especially if you plan to invite women."

"OK, then how about Niger or Chad?"

"Niger same thing. But Chad. Now that could work. Christians from the South control the Government, and the northern part, the Sahara, is Muslim. But not the radicalized Muslims. The tribes in the north, primarily the Tubu, are still very conventional, old line, nomadic peoples."

And so it was that we agreed that if I could arrange for 6 participants, Michael would round out the group to 12. Almost like the cast of Plato's banquet, the cast of characters came with such varied and interesting backgrounds as to make it inevitable that during the hours spent walking, or resting from the sun, or savoring the sweet tea at the end of the day, we would explore the many themes that arose along the way. From Mexico, I brought my friends Juan Angel and Ana Mari, both tri-athletes who enjoyed the challenge and discovery of remote places, and whose journeys had taken them from the ice flows of Antarctica where they photographed penguins guarding their young, to the steamy forests of Ruanda to sit in silence with gorillas; Angelica, and her quadrilingual childhood friend Rocio. I also invited Dick, the Chairman of Outward Bound in New Zealand. Dick had started out as a food engineer, had become bored with his life as an employee in a large cereal company, and decided to start his own cereal business. Some thirty years later, with his company now the largest breakfast cereal company in New Zealand, Dick had turned his energies to other pursuits. His outdoor interests lead him to become interested in Outward Bound. And his commitment to social justice led him to run for Mayor of Auckland, a job for which he had no prior political experience. He won, against all odds, and served a six-year term. The other participant from Down Under was Graham, an encyclopedia of information, a veritable Google in the desert. Graham was to surprise us all.

Michael invited Joe, a feisty 83 year old from California, a former Parole Officer, who now spent some 300 days a year travelling to the ends of the earth. She had travelled with Michael before, in the Sudan, and enjoyed the pace of the camels, the rhythm of the day and Michael's conversation. She brought her friend, Haesoon, a Korean lady who had also travelled with camels before, but whose preferred form of holiday travel was by bicycle.

Martin was the third person who had travelled with Michael before. While Graham was the font of information, Martin was the deepest thinker. His painful shyness kept him apart for much of the time, walking alone, his body bent against the wind, lost in thought. But when presented with a puzzle, particularly one involving the sciences (he was a Cambridge University Chemistry professor) or a philosophical question, you could count on Martin to present an original gem of an idea. Finally, Michael invited a young couple that was living in Karen, less than a mile from where I was born. Eugenie is one of those women who, although completely without make-up or artifice, is so stunningly beautiful that you miss a breath when you first see her. But then you realize that her physical beauty is put to shame by the effervescence of her intellect. She must have been a precocious, irrepressibly loquacious child. She told me once, when I commented, goodnaturedly, on her volubility, that her father, a surgeon, would regularly command her "Do shut up child, your incessant torrent of questions will drive me to drink." Eugenie studied Anthropology at Oxford, and was working on a project with the Turkana people of Northern Kenya. Here she met Frederic, a Belgian photographer who works with such institutions as the Gates Foundation and National Geographic. Frederic's looks, too, would stop traffic on Rodeo Drive. A perfect foil and support for Eugenie, his comments were deliberate, and equally insightful.

It was during this trip that I finally connected the dots, and deciphered the call that I had heard on Kilimanjaro, on Christmas Day four years earlier.

—◆—

Thwack, thwack, thwack.

I awake to the sound of Abakar chopping wood for the fire. It's 5.00 am. I turn over to sleep a little more.

Thwack, thwack.

Impossible to sleep. I lie awake in my sleeping bag staring at the stars. Orion was above me when I fell asleep last night, but he has taken his bow and arrows and left toward the west. In his place I see the five stars of Virgo. A new day, a fresh start. I marvel at the clarity of the night, the brilliance of the stars, the silence. I came to the desert to experience silence, to search within my soul those dark areas where silence never penetrates, where noise, frenzy and pressures are always lurking, ready to upset one's daily balance. The stars don't emit noise, but they do exude a certain presence, a calm that permeates the sky and the air. This is why I came.

As I doze fitfully in the pre dawn I hear the chant of the *Fajr*: *La Ilaha Illa Allah. There is no God but Allah. We have awoken, and all of creation has awoken.* Adom leads the camel drivers in prayer. Facing Mecca, toward the east, they kneel, bend forward, and rub their hands and face with sand in recollection of the ritual washing with water that Mohammed prescribed. They stand and recite the Holy verses. They kneel again, kissing the soil, Mother Earth, thanking God for their existence, and seeking his blessings. Adom chants. It is a haunting, repetitious chant, a chant I have heard before in Lamu, in Istanbul, in Cairo and Khartoum. It is the same the world over, wherever devout Muslims gather to pray.

5.20 in the morning. The Hunter from the East has sent his minions ahead, their light blue standards fluttering above them as they ride. Like the clouds of sand that precede the galloping hordes of Attila the Hun; like the dark shadow that blacks out the sun as a swarm of locusts approach the wheat-filled plains; the Hunter's minions spread a cyan light across the eastern sky. As these warriors advance, the stars retreat, disappearing slowly into oblivion. Behind the sky blue cavalry come orange spear-carriers. Spreading out like infantry these troops paint orange an even greater expanse of sky. Dawn is breaking. It is time to emerge from my cocoon and join the camel drivers as they begin their daily rituals. Not just the cocoon of my sleeping bag, but also the cocoon that has surrounded me and protected me in urban, western society

Abakar has prepared heavily sweetened tea. We break bread, and share a few dates. The dates have a brittle, hard skin that we have to break through in order to suck out the soft flesh. I know the bread won't last longer than two more days, so I relish it, even though it is already hard, like croutons. I spread some pungent goat cheese to give it taste and texture.

As the golden disc of the sun breaks over the horizon I rise from breaking fast with the camel drivers and join them in search of the camels that were let free to roam and seek for food last night. Occasionally, when the terrain is miserably inhospitable, and grass or stalks of cram cram are hard to find, the camel drivers will hobble the camels, bending the lower half of one front leg and tying it to the thigh, almost like a cripple begging on the street with one leg severed at the knee. Although the camels grumble terribly at this indignity, they settle down in front of a bush by which they are abandoned, and chomp happily all night, their lower jaws rotating from side to side as they chew. Last night the camels were allowed to roam, only partially hobbled, with their two front legs tied together as in handcuffs, permitting small steps like those of a geisha, but denying the freedom to run. This morning the camels have spread some two or three kilometers from the camp and we set out with the camel drivers to find them and herd them back to camp.

This is the Ennedi, in the northern part of Chad, one of the poorest countries in the world. The Ennedi is a range of rock formations that spreads north into Libya, and includes the Sahara's highest mountain, Emi Kousi, some 3,000 meters high. The rocks rise inexplicably from the desert, towering in fascinating sculptures above the immense expanse of sand that stretches further than the eye can see. We have joined a group of nomads as they walk with their camels from the Arche Guelta to Mogoro, covering some 25 kilometers a day. We are walking, not joining the small bands of tourists who careen through the desert in their Land Cruisers to marvel at the spectacular scenery and to peer at the camel trains and bands of nomads herding camels to market or seeking for water. It is not just that I want to see their world in a different way, to see more, to see it slowly. It's more than that. Like Thoreau, I wish to confront "the essential facts of life", to "live deep and suck out all the marrow of life, to live so sturdily and Spartan-like as to put to rout all that was not life, to drive life into a corner, and reduce it to its lowest terms." I want to feel the air on my cheek, the sand burning under my feet, rubbing in my shoes, scratching on my dry, cracked face. I want to touch the bushes, feel the prick of the cram cram grass and the thorn trees whose needle-like thorns are fodder for hardy camels. I want to hear the groans of camels as they are loaded or hobbled, the braying of the donkeys that we pass in the little nomad villages dotting the route. I want to be overwhelmed by the gesticulating and yelling of camel drivers as a camel loses his load, and bolts in a panic, taking with him fifteen other camels tied behind him in the train. These things one cannot experience from a magic carpet travel or from behind the window of an automobile. I came for all of that. I found it, but I also found much more because, until today, I have not thought about Why. Why do I need to feel this struggle of Man and Nature? Why do I have to be part of the day-to-day life of the nomad in order to understand the desert, in order to learn from this journey?

By 7.30 the camels are loaded and the caravanserai leaves the Arche Guelta. This day I remember clearly. It is my first day walking beside my camel. Later we will not be able to distinguish one day from the next. In the desert we lost track of time. Time means nothing to our nomad companions, and as the days drift by, time becomes irrelevant to me. But I will recall the sense of revelation that came to me as I progressed in this journey through time. Today my heart beats with an extraordinary sense of adventure as twenty-one camels set sail, some tied in line, others merely following the lead camel. I am Columbus with La Niña, La Pinta and La Santa Maria. I am Burton departing Bagamoyo with two hundred porters. I am Shackelton on the edge of the Antarctic, *"safe return doubtful"*. The air is still early-morning fresh, and all around us are amazing rock formations. What touches me most? Is it the rocks, the vast distances, or the exoticness of the camels, beasts whose ungainly features seem more attuned to a Neolithic world long gone? Or is it the silence, the calm, the absence of anything motorized? Or maybe the people with whom I have chosen to travel, men whose way of life has remained unaltered through centuries, before recorded time.

Last night I heard an owl hoot as the moon rose over the cliffs of the Arche Guelta. But today, no birds sing. Instead, the rocks call out to us. Their shapes come alive: an iguana with his little horns and serrated cockscomb; a pair of Allah's eyes watching as we pass; one hundred virgins guarding a tomb; elephant trunks and camels' feet. All of these appear to me in the rock formations as we walk.

I have come to grow closer to Nature. This too I will achieve, but still there will be more. We see the dung beetles living on the dung of camels and goats. We see the tiny desert mice whose large eyes and ears distinguish them, but whose true secret is their ability to survive without water. We see the tracks of snakes in the sand, and, as I explore the caves for pre-historic art, I see their eyes, their frightened teeth and nervous tongues as they curl up deep in the caves fearful of my predatory power. We see the fennec foxes, their pelts as white and soft brown as the sands themselves, the foxes that hunt mice and snakes, and feed on fallen birds. We marvel at the grace and speed of the gazelles as they streak across the desert like flashes of light in a sand storm. And we hear the baying of the hyenas that are the lords of the food chain in the desert. But, I ask myself: "Is this Nature? What is Nature, what is it that I love? Are these species of animals the Nature I came to see and to feel? Or is there more?"

The sun is now beating hard on the caravanserai. The pace slows a little. The camels are ungainly, but walk with a grace that is astonishing, the soft hoof of the back right foot landing inches from the rising hoof of the front left foot. There is a rhythm to how they walk, and the camel drivers sing to the camels when they ride, singing in unison with the rhythm of their stride. The nomad's life is constructed around his relationship with his camels and his environment. I came to be close to Nature, but Michael tells me that in order to get close to Nature I should understand the life of the nomad, and his symbiotic relationship with nature. Michael's two great heroes are Lawrence of Arabia and William Thesiger. Researching his book, *Lawrence, the Uncrowned King of Arabia*, Michael travelled in the footsteps of Lawrence, stood in the hills and fortresses where Lawrence stood, and imagined himself in Lawrence's shoes. But, here in Ennedi, Michael lives and breathes Thesiger, Thesiger who explored all this part of the Sahara and wrote *The Life of my Choice*, his travelogue of these parts. Michael knew Thesiger when he retired to Maralal in northern Kenya, and wrote the definitive biography of Thesiger. He tells me that one of Thesiger's lasting laments was that: "We destroy the things we love." In Thesiger's case his sadness came from his infatuation with beautiful nomadic boys whom he showered with affection and gifts, but who became spoiled, comfortable, no longer pristine, infected by the sins of the occidental world, and turned against Thesiger in his old age. Michael's lament is that Man is at war with Nature, constantly trying to tame Nature, to conquer Nature, rather than learning how to live with Nature. "When Man finally wins his war against Nature," he tells me, echoing Schumacher, "he will find himself on the losing side." "These men," he continues, referring to the camel drivers and their families, "are among the few people left on earth whose life is truly sustainable. They are not destroying Nature to build their world. They are not exhausting their water resources. They are not stripping the planet of its oil, its uranium, its forests and rivers. They have all they need to live, and their mode of living gives back to Nature so she can replenish herself." Michael is a philosopher, a *"Deep Ecologist"*, a member of a movement founded by Arne Naess, and supported by ardent followers around the world. "The Touareg and the Tubu, the Kababish and the Goran, they have lived in the Sahara since time immemorial," he tells me, "but the Sahara was not always thus."

At Arche, Michael had shown us rock art painted on the walls of a ceremonial platform. He explained how some 6,000 to 9,000 years ago, the Sahara was a lush savannah, populated by animals now found only in sub-Saharan Africa: antelope, elephant, crocodiles and lion. During this period the inhabitants of the Sahara progressed from being purely hunter/gatherers, to being pastoralists. About 4,000 BC the Sahara began a warming phase, leading, ultimately, to a move to the Nile and the arrival of camels and a nomadic culture in the Saharan desert some twenty five hundred years ago. On the third day, at Oadi Totor, our Tubu guides had pointed us toward a cave that contained more drawings and scratchings. Upon discovering this second cave there is an explosion of ideas, of theories, of hypotheses to explain this find. "This is a camel running," says Frederic. "I see an antelope," replies Eugenie, "look here at these little horns. And anyway camels don't run like that." "Agreed," comments Graham, "but as recently as two hundred years ago our occidental artists were drawing horses running with all four legs extended. We should not expect more from a primitive artist lying on his back scratching at a rock with another rock blade." Michael reminds us that camels did not populate this land until twenty five hundred years ago and that these paintings were clearly older than that. "They depict shamanistic activity," says Michael, who is also an avid supporter of the theories of Terence McKenna, the anthropologist who first articulated the proposition that the early Saharans followed shamanistic practices, often induced by ceremonies with hallucinogenic mushrooms. At which point Eugenie triumphantly points out that there are two layers of art. The first is a layer of painting, in a red paint and with a slim brush stroke, mostly depicting the pastoral stage some six thousand years ago. The second layer, which in some cases is superimposed above the painted art, is a layer of petroglyphs, scratched into the rock and still white against the rock's brown background. This layer, she points out, is newer, and depicts the shift from a pastoral to a nomadic, camel herding culture.

As the hubbub subsides and moves to the lunch mat, I lie alone in the cave. I see parallel curved lines in the sand indicating the presence of a snake in the cave with me, but I know he is curled up in a deep corner far from where I will venture. I look out from the cave over miles of desert sand, dotted with the rock formations I have come to call my friends. I imagine an early pastoralist lying here, the sun setting to his right, his cattle grazing below, and I wonder why he chose to paint here. I see the figures of men with long heads, maybe mushroom heads, and the chess board-like markings in the stomachs of several of the cows, and I give more credence to Michael's ideas of shamans and rituals being depicted in a sacred place. There are no answers, only mysteries.

That evening, Michael was concerned. His GPS showed us travelling about 26 km a day. His contacts in Chad, who had set up the logistics of the expedition, had told him we would need to travel 30 km a day. He was afraid we would reach Mogoro a day late, miss our pick-up and miss our flights home. He decided to discuss the matter with Kalé, the oldest of our nomad companions, that evening after dinner. Kalé was a man of undeterminable age, probably between forty and sixty. He had started to put on a little weight, unlike the other five men who tended to the camels. Kalé lived in a small hut made of mud and wattle, not far from a well that we passed on the third day, and introduced us to his family, two wives and a handful of jet black children who respectfully, or maybe timidly, kept their distance as we appeared. They had never seen white people, Kalé told us. Kalé was not a talkative man. He preferred to keep his peace and leave the talking to Saleh, a man in his early thirties who had served in the Chadian army and had a familiarity with the quirks of the white man's world. The other four members of the nomad team were barely out of their teens. They would run ahead, play games with sticks and rocks, chatter, hold hands and giggle, like schoolboys. For them this expedition was a hilarious diversion from their daily routine.

The conversation with Kalé and Saleh did not go well that evening. "Of course we will arrive at Mogoro by 10 in the morning, Wednesday," they confirmed. Michael pulled out a map. "What is that well called?........OK, and where will we get to tomorrow? …. And the next day….?" What seemed like a fairly simple presentation of the route of the expedition, and the timetable, dissolved into endless discussions of names of rocks, the heat of the day, the need for the camels to have a two hour break at lunch, whether we could walk faster, what time to start walking in the morning, and on and on. Gradually, we drifted off to bed, leaving Michael (talking with Kalé in Arabic), and Frederic (getting into more heated argument with Saleh in French). Nothing was resolved that evening, other than a commitment to start walking a little earlier in the morning.

As the next day started, our group waited expectantly for signs of increased urgency from our companions. The morning prayers came and went as usual. Tea and cereal appeared, were consumed and packed away. Two of the younger lads went sent in search of the camels, but the others stayed behind. The first worrying sign. Instead of the cheerful, childlike behavior we were used to, the large smiles, the friendly greetings and handshakes, the Tubu men were sullen and reserved. It was clear that we would be starting later, much later than usual. This was what the British call a "work stoppage" or a "go slow". Not quite a strike, but enough to bring the transport system to an infuriatingly snail-like pace that causes gridlock in the city. It did not take long for us to realize that we had no leverage, no negotiating power at all. If our Tubu guides decided to leave us, we had no idea how to return or to advance, we had no food or water other than that which was carried on their camels. Although we had an idea where we were, using GPS, we had no way of making contact with anyone, and our maps were rudimentary at best. And no one had passed our way in the three days in which we had travelled.

As the sun began to rise, Michael and Frederic sat down again with Kalé and Saleh. This time, all the younger men were asked to step aside, and we retreated to what little shade we could find. For the better part of two hours the men discussed. Michael laid out stones in the sand to represent rock formations and stopping points. Kalé named the rocks, the wells and the oases along the way. None of it made sense. Our maps showed different names. Michael's itinerary indicated a greater distance than would be covered walking 7 ½ hours a day at an average of 3½ kilometers an hour. At one particularly heated juncture, Frederic, exasperated at the lack of progress, told Michael: "Tell them that we have money, and that if we arrive on time we will give them extra money. But if we are late they get nothing." Saleh's response was immediate and spoken with disdain: "Money, what is money? We don't know money. It means nothing to us." Michael declined to push the point further. He knew his nomadic comrades too well. Eventually, a truce was reached, but clearly we had no choice but to travel at their pace. And to trust them. Another mental adjustment. From now on we could not even attempt to trace where we were on the map, the map that was about as useful as the old charts the Spanish explorers drew to mark the trail they had followed from the sea to the land of gold mines and temples. We had to put aside the count of days, and accept that we might be here six days more or eight days. Time could no longer be a dimension that had measurable beginnings and endings, other than the measure of a day, from sun up to sun down.

That evening the sunset had a particularly poignant feel to it. We had stopped without sheltering rocks or bushes nearby. The wind had picked up, galloping south from the Mongolian steppes, across the frigid Syrian desert, and, unbroken, was now hitting our caravanserai. It had a sharp, bitter cold bite to it, penetrating my fleece jacket and making me wish I was better prepared. Our group was subdued, the usual camaraderie and banter missing. Eugenie broke the silence:

"What do you think Saleh meant when he said *What is money, We don't know money*? Of course they know what money is, and he especially since he has served in the army."

She had her head on Frederic's broad shoulder, resting there, protected. Frederic is a big man, both powerful and gentle. He responded first, the others less eager to take up the theme.

"Saleh spoke in French when he made that comment. He said: *Nous ne connaissons pas l'argent*. When we use *connaitre* like that it might mean to know, or it might mean to be familiar with. Maybe he is saying that we don't use money."

"Of course they are familiar with money. How do they acquire the clothes they are wearing, if not with money?" Rocio asks.

Graham leans forward, his expressive face alive with the seeds of an idea. "Michael, who owns the land they live on?" he asks.

"No-one and everyone. Kalé has no more right to place his hut on that spot of land we saw, than the next man. Nor any less right."

"And the water?" continues Graham.

"The same. Water is a communal possession. Allah gives water to all mankind, and no-one may store it for his personal use to the exclusion of others."

"And what about the camels. I am guessing that is different because they all seem to have markings?"

"Yes, indeed. Camels are property. The markings tell first what community or family they belong to. Sometimes the markings also identify a single owner, but not always. Camels are undoubtedly the nomad's most important possession, and they are treated with care and respect."

To which Frederic interjects: "Which is why we have to wait two hours at midday while their camels graze. The health of their camels is more important than anything else for these guys." Frederic is bothered by the fact that our guides don't get the fact that they are here on a job, paid by us to accomplish a certain goal. It irks him that it is more important to Kalé that his camels are as fat the day they arrive in Mogoro as the day they left, than that we achieve our goal.

Graham rocks backward, tossing his hair out of his face. He continues his line of questioning: "And do they buy and sell camels? Do they use money to acquire this important possession?"

"Occasionally. But typically they raise the camels they have, and don't buy or sell. There are some markets, and I have been to them, where the nomads travel from hundreds of miles to trade camels for food or clothing, but it is normally barter not cash, although, of course, cash does change hands, and, without question, they do understand the concept of money and the value of money."

Turning away from camels for a moment, Rocio, who is a single working mother raising a family, points out that most of what these men carry with them on this trip is made by them.

"The saddles are made from two pieces of wood, found wood, barely worked, but in just the right shape, a Y, to form the base for a saddle. The water is carried in goatskins, stripped of all flesh, dried in the sun, sewn up along the stomach and the legs, leaving only an opening at the head from which they drink. The reins and bridles are made from hide."

"And yet," remarks Angelica, "they also make things that at not utilitarian, things that are purely decorative or beautiful. My camel, Koré Koré, for example, has a beautiful woven amulet hanging from her ear. This was not bought, and I doubt it will be sold. It is purely an amulet, made for art or maybe for love."

"But Kalé's *djelabayah*, the shoes they wear, these are not made by them. And I don't think they went to the market in el Fasher and traded a camel for a *djelabayah*. He bought that with cash." says Rocio, ever the pragmatist.

Dick stirs from his Roman Senator repose. He is not good at sitting cross-legged like a young yoga teacher. Too many years climbing mountains, I suspect. "Maybe the important question" he says, entering the conversation for the first time, "is not whether they know what money is, nor whether they use it occasionally or regularly, but whether they are motivated by money. In my business, I have learned that you can't always motivate people with money. Some people stay with you because they like the culture of the workplace. Others value flexibility in their schedule, or time off in which they can travel."

At which point Michael, who has been unusually quiet during the discussion, jumps back in. After all, he lived with nomads in the Sahara for three years, he speaks perfect Arabic and several dialects used by the various tribes. He knows these men like he knows his brother. He has changed from his daytime *djelabayah*, a greyish cloth trimmed with red, set off with a red and white checked headdress. This evening he is wearing cream, a softer look.

"These nomads, these Tubu tribesmen, have a code of honor that involves five characteristics: Courage, Hospitality, Generosity, Endurance and Loyalty. These are the things that are important to them. Dick is right. They are not motivated by money. For us occidentals, money has become not just a tool that enables us to trade for the necessities of life. Nor is it merely a tool to trade for the luxuries of life. Money has become a symbol, a symbol of who I am, how important I am, how marriageable I am. For these men, money does not have that meaning. It does not motivate them. Like us, they are motivated by the respect they receive in their community, but that respect has nothing to do with their wealth. It has everything to do with how they act. They will share their meals, their rugs, even their humble homes with you. Even if a man is my enemy, I am required to offer him food and shelter for three days, and then, if he is foe, he must be given twenty four hours lead time before I can pursue him again."

Haesoon joins the fray. Although not what Michael refers to as an "occidental", she lives near Seoul, a city as capitalist and modern as any Western city. But, she is a Buddhist, and her home is by a river outside of town, a peaceful, simple place, far from the center of town. She speaks a broken English that is hard to understand, but always worth listening to.

"I agree with Michael" she says. "We become attach to things because we afraid, because we not at peace with ourself or with our true value. Our community send mix signals about what is value, and instead of living according to Code of action, like these Tubu, we attach to things. But what we miss is that the true spring of wealth is in Self. From the Self we find the strength, the consciousness, to find peace. Everything else is a symbol. Brand name clothes. Sports cars. Big, big houses with many rooms and balcony. These things do not bring us peace. They leave us empty. They have no soul."

Silence. Even Eugenie is temporarily without words. There is something about the way Buddhists speak and express themselves that leaves "occidentals" at a loss, especially the Puritan Work Ethic occidentals. They start from such a different place. It's like playing football (soccer) on the beach. You can't dribble and feint. The ground is different, the way of thinking is different, linking up and communicating is different.

Angelica, who has grown close to Haesoon on the walks, and shares many of her sensibilities, poses the question: "Do you think this has anything to do with reincarnation?"

"What are you talking about, my dear?" I ask. I am not making the connection between big houses and reincarnation, and I don't think anyone else is, but they don't know her well enough to know that it is not just a random comment.

"Well, the Greeks, actually the Athenians, in particular Socrates and Plato, believed in a kind of Ethos of Exceptionalism, by which they referred to every man's (yes they primarily talked about men, not women), every man's ability to be exceptional, to rise up from ordinariness, to make a mark in life. This Ethos got lost in the European Middle Ages when thought or philosophy was controlled by the Church, and individual achievement was not valued as it was by the Greeks or by us. Now, in the West, we enter a phase in which much of society is god-less, or at least not philosophically directed by a Church, and I think that the need to make a mark, to prove oneself exceptional, is praised, and rewarded in our society."

The Cult of Individualism occurs to me but I am puzzled and not thinking laterally. "And so?" I ask. "And so how does the Church and reincarnation fit in?"

Haesoon got it immediately. "Of course, Angelica, it is relevant. We Buddhists are not worried about the mark we make in the world. Our sense of existence on this planet is not so temporary. Since we believe in reincarnation, we know we will come around again and again. Yes, it is important that we live spiritual lives, that we are connected with the other inhabitants of the earth, the animals, the birds, the land and nature, so that we are in a good place when we return in the next life, but we have no need to have or show wealth on earth." Haesoon shuffles a little, maybe uncomfortable at being the center of attention.

Martin leans across to me: "Methinks she speaks of Walt Whitman: 'demented with the mania of owning things'."

Haesoon continues after a pause: "Michael, our guides are Muslims. They don't believe in reincarnation, do they?"

"No Haesoon, they don't, but their religion is important to them and relevant to Angelica's point about the Ethos of Exceptionalism. These people, and most Sahara nomads, their lives revolve around the five prayers a day, and their rigid set of customs. They have a value-system, which, as I explained, is geared entirely to the community. They have no need, no wish, to be Exceptional. They have what Nature gives them and they ask no more. They don't try to tame Nature. They are in a symbiotic relationship with Nature. They use what she offers, and never take more than they need. They do not deplete Nature."

Graham has been sitting quietly for a while, his mind wandering since Angelica introduced Plato. We find out later that, among Graham's many encyclopedic references are the works of Plato, whom he greatly admires.

"Do you think these peoples' sense of time is relevant to the discussion?" he asks. "I mean, that's what we were arguing about, after all. How much time will it take to get to Mogoro? They don't care about time. They measure each day by the sun rising and falling. They barely have seasons. They have no deadlines. Maybe the fact that there is no pressure to be "Exceptional" gives them the freedom to enjoy the day. You know, Plato has an example in one of his dialogues. He compares a lawyer who is running to and from the courts, with a philosopher or a student. The latter, says Plato, talks peacefully. His time is his own. He can discuss a theme, and then when another person joins the group he can move to another theme or bring the newcomer in. The lawyer, says Plato, is like a slave, his time is not his own. But the philosopher is a free man. Maybe these nomads are the only free men camped here under these beautiful stars tonight."

"No doubt more free than me," comments Rocio. "I certainly don't feel free when I'm at home. Two children in University, clients who have deadlines, that's not freedom."

"Are their women free?" asks Eugenie. "I haven't seen any of them hanging out relaxing under the shade of a rock. And from what little I remember of having to read Plato in our first year at University, the Athenian women did not have too much freedom either."

"That, my dear Eugenie," interjects Dick, "is a whole other question, and we are getting into, shall we say, "shifting sands" with that topic." Dick always enjoyed the suggestion of a pun. "It has been a long day, and I am headed to my sleeping bag and my little area under the stars."

With that, the group agreed to call it a night and to resume the conversation in the morning. As Angelica and I lay awake, reading Thesiger aloud, headlamps on our foreheads, she paused on this sentence from *Life of my Choice:* "In the desert I had found a freedom unattainable in civilization; a life unhampered by possession, since everything that was not a necessity was an encumbrance." "Our conversation this evening about the freedom of these nomads," she began, "it's not really about the pressures of daily western life, its not about whether a woman can chose her man, its not about the Taliban and French fries, its about waking to the sun, walking hand in hand with your childhood friend, simply being part of the natural world in the same way as an eagle, or a fox or the wind is part of that world." That night I scribbled in my journal a verse that came to me, that captured the sense of freedom I felt that day, a new found freedom, like that of the butterfly emerging from his cocoon:

> *Burning heat and biting cold*
> *Spirit young though limbs grow old*
> *Unencumbered, unconstrained*
> *Sahara, Freedom is thy name.*

CHAPTER 17

DIALOGUES IN THE DESERT

One of the joys of walking in the Sahara is the rhythm of the day. There is no way in which Plato's lawyer would survive here, unless he flicked the switch and changed his pace. There is a deliberateness to the day. As one sets off, with the morning air still cold, the distance ahead of you is immense, interminable. I think of the Boers trekking up from South Africa to Kenya. I think of Lewis and Clark. I think of the Jews returning to Israel, led by Moses. But there is time to talk. This day Angelica and Rocio fall in with Graham as I join Michael and Frederic at the front of the caravanserai. Graham was definitely unique on the expedition. In addition to having an encyclopedic mind, and occasionally holding forth at length on the most abstruse aspects of an answer to a simple question, Graham held other mysteries. He was a large, strong man, about 3 inches above 6 foot, and with the arms and shoulders of a man who used to lift weights. But his muscles were no longer toned. They had taken on a softness that suggested a change in lifestyle. Graham wore his hair long and grew no beard. The prior evening Graham joined us for dinner wearing a pair of purple shoes that slipped over his large feet like slippers, and then retired to a purple sleeping bag. That morning as he walked with Angelica and Rocio he asked them "Would you call me Ivy? I am more comfortable with Ivy than Graham. Graham was my given name, and although my parents still call me that, my friends call me Ivy."

Graham was in the process of changing his body from being that of a male to that of a woman. "I am a woman in a man's body, and I need to change my body to be aligned with my soul" he confided. Angelica and Rocio had liked Graham from the beginning. They appreciated his considerateness, his sensitivity, his connectedness. Now they embraced Ivy, and gave her a hug of support.

That evening we felt the temperature dropping fast. More Siberian winds were approaching and we needed to find a place to camp before darkness fell. We had learned that our nomad guides were wont to simply stop where they were as night fell, but that evening we urged them to find sheltered ground. Walking ahead I spot a group of rocks whose U shaped configuration promises protection even if the wind direction shifts, and I prevail on my comrades to head toward them in the hopes that they will provide the shelter we sought.

The spot is off the traditional path taken by these men and their ancestors for centuries, but they agree, and shortly before nightfall a halt is called under the shadow of these U shaped rocks. In sharp contrast to the gentle, methodical pace of the day's march, the camp is now a hive of activity. Abakar finds some dead wood and starts a fire. Abdullai boils a large pot of water for couscous, and chops the onions, cabbage and other hardy vegetables that he has been transporting, preparing the dinner. The camel drivers unload the camels and lay out their rugs, praying before the sun goes down, the penultimate prayer of the day. We expeditioners spread out to find suitable sites to pitch tent or sleep under the stars. But wait, a hoot of discovery from Frederic. His usual calm demeanour is shed and he is grinning from ear to ear. He calls to Michael to run over. He has found wonderful petroglyphs, three large drawings of what can only be mushrooms, carved into the rock wall. Is this the proof Michael was looking for, proof that this was indeed a shamanistic culture, inspired by hallucinogenic mushrooms? The petroglyphs are some two feet tall, unequivocally mushroom shaped, and bearing the same chess board-like markings as the bodies of the camels at Oadi Totor. Close by are more carvings in the wall. Two figures, men with mushroom-like heads, holding in one hand something like the infinity symbol, or a figure 8, with their heads connected to the horns of a seated cow or antelope. What are these images? Do their head shapes indicate a hallucinogenic state? Are they connected spiritually to the cows, or are they sacrificing them? A thousand questions, with almost as many answers. But one thing is for sure: Our expedition has stumbled upon unmistakable evidence of the presence of primitive man; not just primitive man, but a society that had the time and inclination to depict complex social activity, probably sacred activity, and most likely related to the shamanistic practices that McKenna argues existed in the desert. Michael tells us that in all his readings on the hallucinogenic mushrooms of the Sahara he has never seen pictures of these carvings, and thinks they may be a new discovery.[8]

As night falls the wind drops and the night is clear and warm. Angelica and I sleep on an altar below some minor petroglyphs and I dream of pastoral man wandering in a grassy, luxurious meadow that is now the desert. I recall the story that Saint-Exupéry tells in *Wind, Sand and Stars*. He recounts how, many decades ago, when the French first established bases in the Sahara, they invited three nomadic elders to visit France, to be amazed at the wonders that modern man had created. These men were not impressed by the Champs Elysees, nor by the Eiffel Tower, nor the cars and steam engines. They took it as a given that their French hosts could create such things. Instead they marveled at the trees. They stood astonished before a waterfall, believing themselves in the presence of the Almighty. They knew of the existence of such things, but only from the Koran, where it is written that if we live a life of hardship and sacrifice and virtue, God will reward us with Paradise, a place where trees grow large and shady, where water flows in unending rivers, and birds sing. But they did not talk of these things upon their return to the desert and to their fellow tribesmen because they felt betrayed by their God. How could their God demand so much of them, and provide them with so little, when the God of the French rewarded Frenchmen with paradise on earth. These things, says Saint-Exupéry, were better not discussed with their comrades in the desert. I realized, that night, that our comrades, the Tubu camel drivers, would not understand if I were to tell them that I live in a box set upon another box, on another box, on another box. Forty box houses set one upon another. That from the window of my box I can see across a space wide enough for eight camels to walk side by side, but then my view is limited by more boxes where people live. They would not understand if I were to tell them that where I live, people are born and die without ever seeing the sun rise or fall below the horizon; or that there is never Silence, but always some noise created by Man. The noise of a blaring horn, of a truck slowing its descent with its engine, of an ambulance siren ripping the night air. They would not understand that where they see stars and rocks and sand, I see billboards shouting at me to buy this device or to look like that person because a film star's face is staring at me. I fall asleep realizing that the essence of this journey was not a journey through the sands, but a journey through time, a journey back to a world in which Man was in harmony with Nature, not at war, and I vow to take whatever small steps I can to stop the destruction of the thing we love.

But my journey is not over. I still have two more lessons to learn. On our penultimate evening with the camels, we reach Anoa, an almost mythical oasis at the foot of a towering rock. Against the rock, on its lee side, sheltered from the wind, an enormous pyramid of sand has formed, its edge a perfect line, sharply defined and silhouetted by the setting sun. Golden brown on its westward edge. Dark and shaded on its eastern side below the ridge line. At the foot of this sand pyramid lie date palms, swaying gently in the evening breeze. And beside the date palms, a lake, an oasis. Angelica and I walk silently, reverentially, hand in hand, to this special place. As we sit with the sun dropping behind us, the sand hill golden, the rock face deep brown, the water of the oasis bronzed and gently rippling, some black winged stilts glide in, their long red legs stretched straight behind them like the fuselage of an ancient airplane. They are joined by a pair of wood ducks, and then another and another, always in pairs. Finally, with the sun dropping, burning into the desert sand, swallows appear, dashing, darting, swooping as they catch the flies and bugs that are in the air. How do these birds get here? Do they live here year round, or are they messengers from Europe, migrating south and merely passing through?

The next morning, Angelica and I are back by the oasis before dawn, to watch the sun rise and to imprint the beauty of this place forever in our mind. The ducks and stilts are not there when we arrive. They have found another place to spend the night, but they will arrive soon. We set out to walk around the oasis, a circumnavigation of sorts, a way to capture the totality of this serene spot. About half the way around, a narrow stream leads into the date palms. We follow this, expecting to find a path around the lake. Instead, in a shaded place, set apart from the oasis, but connected by this stream, we find a crystal clear pool. I touch the water. The water in the oasis lake is cold this predawn morn, but this pool is warm. I strip down and lie there, warmed and cleansed by water from the depths of the earth. Mother Earth.

We recall a well we passed on our journey. This well was in the middle of miles of sand desert, without geographical formation or other clue to its existence that we could observe. Four bore holes, each over a hundred meters deep, have been dug side by side, like the points of a compass. Groups of camels, many numbering thirty or more, are standing around while their owners fill huge leather-skinned bags with water. Four bags are being filled at once, each dropped in a different borehole. The bags fall the hundred meters attached to a rope that feeds through a pulley and is attached to a camel, which then walks away in the direction of the relevant compass point, raising the water to hand. This process is repeated again and again, all day long, pulling water up from the depths of the earth. It occurs to me as I lie in the warm spring water that this well has been there since time immemorial. That it has provided the most sacred essence, the stuff of Paradise, to these nomads since before they were nomads, when they were bringing their cattle here to graze. That like the crystalline water in which I am luxuriating, this water is a gift from the Gods, not sent down from Heaven, but brought up from Mother Earth. This water is the umbilical chord that ties these camel drivers to Nature, a Nature that is much broader and much more profound than my image of Nature, that of animals and birds, trees and shrubs. This is, as Kalidasa wrote, *"the very life of life."*

That afternoon Eugenie found some remnants of ostrich shells. She approached Kalé.

"Are there ostriches here?" she asks, holding out the shell.

"No longer," he replies, through Michael, who interprets, "they were all killed in the war," referring to the series of skirmishes between Chad and Libya over the rights to the ninety kilometer wide strip known as the Aouzou, that lasted for nearly a decade, ending in 1987.

"How were they killed?" she asks, "I have no doubt they did not take sides in the skirmishes." Kalé smiles his toothless grin.

"The soldiers are not from here. They were from the cities, and from the south. They know nothing of the desert. They drive around in Land Cruisers with nothing to do. They have AK 47s, and it is fun to chase ostriches. Also, you can feed forty people on one ostrich."

"Just killing time, huh" mutters Eugenie.

"Yes, the last ostriches were killed when I was still a young man."

In the evening, Ana Mari and Frederic display their trove of found artifacts, fragments of pottery, stones of various colors, rocks chiseled into representative shapes. Eugenie pulls out her ostrich shell remnants and asks Michael what the war was about.

"Gaddafi claimed that Libya had some ancient right to the Aouzou region, but in reality, he wanted access to the uranium, which is rich in that area. The French rely heavily on nuclear power, and obtain most of their uranium from Chad. So they armed the Chadian forces and ensured that the uranium stayed in Chadian hands."

"Of course," comments Frederic, "the real tragedy lies not just in the loss of ostriches from this area, the beauty of a male and female pair trotting gracefully across the horizon like a pair of dhows at sunset. Nor is it the part they play in the ecology of the region, providing a source of protein to snakes, mice, vultures, and so on. But, from a human perspective, the Tubu now do not have the ostrich feathers that have been part of their heritage for generations, nor do they have the ostrich skin that they have used to make sandals, or the shells from which they create the beautiful necklaces that we saw on the women in the market at Abeche."

At this, Michael becomes animated, even more animated than usual, and jumping into the conversation, he exclaims:

"Exactly. The way these men, these soldiers, acted, is simply not sustainable. I mean, if we all act this carelessly in our relationship to Nature, there will be no Nature left. And, mark my words, we will regret that."

Ivy, who has discussed Michael's views on Deep Ecology with him during the expedition, comments, quietly: "If I am not mistaken, Michael, that sounds a lot like the Deep Ecology platform."

"Yes, it is. Humans, animals, and indeed all forms of life, have an equal right to exist on this planet. We have no right to treat them, and all of Nature, as somehow our personal domain."

This comment shocks me. It seems way too radical to support the conclusions about Man's relationship with Nature that I espouse.

"Hang on, Michael. On what do you support your proposition about our rights, or the rights of animals? It sounds dogmatic, and similar in tone to the kind of religious nostrums that both you and

I reject as being unfounded and misleading. Indeed, if we were to start from what we know about the animal world, we might come to the opposite conclusion. Might is right, and survival of the fittest, are the rules of Nature. Not just for animals, but for insects, reptiles, even plants as well. I don't see why we should come to a different conclusion for the rights and obligations of humanity."

"Even if we accept that survival of the fittest is some kind of universal law, Julian, it does not support the action of these soldiers," comments Frederic who has spent weeks in the wild photographing animals, and has a good sense of their behavior. "Sure, a lioness will kill to eat and to feed her family; a silverback gorilla will attack any intruder who threatens his sole access to alpha females, but they won't act randomly. They won't attack without reason. This behavior is also exhibited at the tribal level. Bands of chimpanzees will attack other bands if they enter the first band's territory, but they won't attack without some need to protect resources."

Ivy suggests a compromise position. "Julian, how would you feel about a modified version of Michael's statement? Something along the lines of: While we may be the most powerful species on earth, Natural Law would suggest that we should use that power only as necessary to meet our needs."

"I like it" I reply, and Michael nods his assent.

"But," continues Ivy, two steps ahead of me, "If we say, 'we <u>should</u> use that power only as necessary to meet our needs', what is the source of the obligation? What is it that commands, or directs, that we <u>should</u> act in a certain way? Is the obligation some kind of ethical obligation or are we suggesting, by the reference to Natural Law, that it is more than that?"

"It is both," observes Michael. "It's both an ethical obligation and the result of an evolved self interest. As Frederic pointed out, although these soldiers had fun, and enjoyed the feast of ostrich meat; and although they then returned to their urban ghettos where the extinction of ostriches from the Ennedi meant nothing to them; they have made life for the Tubu tribesmen that much less sustainable. If everyone acted like these soldiers, and, by the way, I think most members of the western world act precisely in this manner, very soon the world is a less livable place for all of us."

"Hold on Mate," interjects Dick, "I don't know if you include New Zealand as part of your western world, Michael, but I think you are being overbroad in your attack on our modern society." Dick has been a successful businessman, and has plowed much of his wealth back into ecological projects. In addition to his commitment to Outward Bound, Dick has supported wilderness space and outdoor recreation for many years in New Zealand.

"I, and, I believe, a majority of us Kiwis, have a strong commitment to the environment. You won't see us driving gas-guzzling cars. We recycle where we can. We avoid the heavy industry that produces global warming. I think we are very conscious of our footprint in the world."

"With all due respect Dick, and I do respect both your views and your undoubted commitment, I think that you and most environmentalists have got it wrong. If a water pipe breaks in your bathroom, do you set about mopping up the flooding with rags and buckets, or do you get in there and seal the pipe? In my view, our society is tolerating the broken pipe and trying to minimize the damage with mops and Band-Aids. The problem is that somewhere in the past, possibly as long ago as a thousand years, but certainly as little as 150 years ago, with the advent of the Industrial Revolution, Man began to decimate Nature at a rate much faster than that at which Nature could replace itself. And, to make matters worse, in many cases, Man did this not because of a necessity, but because of greed, because of a wish to demonstrate wealth or power, because of attachment to things, often things that he did not need, but which were symbols. As Haesoon said, today we see families with several homes, all of them with five bedrooms, over 5,000 square feet, with numerous cars, and mechanical toys, and on and on… That is what is not sustainable. We have to change the way Man thinks about his relationship with Nature, and, unfortunately, that is becoming increasingly difficult because, more and more, Man has no relationship with Nature. People live in cities or huge suburban sprawls, and never come close to understanding what their consuming habits are doing to the rest of the world. Consumerism is destroying the world because now we consume for the sake of consuming."

"Indeed," comments Ivy, "what we have seen here in the desert is a society that views Nature, and its resources, as a partner in their community, not as a storehouse of resources for the use and profit of humanity, free to be taken, used, abused, and exhausted. We don't have the right to ransack these resources willy-nilly."

"Willy-nilly?" asks Haesoon. "What's that?"

"Oh, sorry. As if these resources were endless, and that Man, as the most powerful of the animals, has no accountability for destroying these resources, regardless of the cost to the other species on the planet."

"Or to future generations" adds Eugenie. "I wonder whether my children will see and marvel at elephants grazing peacefully in the wild."

"Or, to steal from Thoreau," I muse, "*will they come to this world like a person picking up a book, only to find that their ancestors have torn out many of the first leaves and grandest passages?*"

The group is tired and conversation flags. The next day is our last day with the camels and we all want to retire early to write in our journals, to think over the path we have travelled. I had come to grow closer to Nature, but now I realized that there is nothing to come close to: I am part of Nature, just as I am part of the Nihill family, of the Colonial tribe, of Humanity. If I see Nature, or wilderness, as an Other, if I try to tame Nature, I am destroying myself. This is my identity.

———

Returning to Mexico, I was struck by a large billboard on the road from the Monterrey airport to my hotel. This billboard sat atop a 40 foot steel tube anchored in the rock of the hill that divides the City of Monterrey from the adjacent town of Garza Garcia. The steel had been fabricated from iron extracted from an iron mine in Jalisco, Mexico. We consume almost 2 billion tons of iron a year, second only to petroleum in the volume of raw material consumed annually. Mexico produces some 14% of this worldwide production. The process of producing steel starts with a mine in Jalisco, Mexico, where enormous drilling machines blast a hole sixty feet deep into the bedrock. Explosives are then dropped into these holes so that large areas of rock substrate become unstable and pliable for other machines to extract iron ore. This iron ore is then loaded onto trucks and transported to kilns where huge furnaces are stoked to a temperature of 1,200 degrees. These furnaces are run on electricity generated in the rain forests of Mexico and transmitted hundreds of miles across Mexico to the kilns. Emerging from the kilns, the molten iron ire is formed into steel tubes, laminated and prepared for shipment. Arriving in Monterrey on the beds of huge double bed trucks, these forty-foot pillars are stored in a warehouse where metal workers bolt the enormous cages of steel and wire that will provide the frame for the billboard. Once that construction is done, the tubes, with their steel cages attached, are again transported by truck to the crest of the ridge between Monterrey and Garza Garcia where they will be erected. This next step is not simple. Before the billboard is erected, a hole twelve feet deep and three feet wide must be dug by another machine, a "digger", which is also loaded onto the back of a pickup truck. In order to dig a hole of this size, the digger needs to clear an area some fifty feet wide, removing all trees and bushes in the area. At this point a gang of laborers is brought up to the billboard site, and there begins a complex process of lifting the steel pillar, assisted by a crane, positioning it in the hole and filling the hole with concrete. The bare billboard is stabilized with wire stays anchored in cement posts dug into the rock, and the billboard company's salesman's job begins, to find someone eager to advertise.

It was not just the size of the billboard that struck me, nor was it the reflections on all that had gone into bringing me this piece of advertising that would hopefully catch my imagination and cause me to spend money on a product that I may or may not need, but that surely I would want having seen the display. It was the item displayed. This enormous billboard displayed a young woman, from mid torso to the knees, leaning back on a sofa with one leg bent and the other extended, wearing delicate, lacey underwear. I was struck by the incongruity of the display of this delicate, intimate product on the highest point of the hill between the two metropolitan areas of Mexico's second city, the incongruity of the iron ore and rock, and furnaces and trucks and laborers that had erected the display, with the softness, the delicacy, the fineness of the product. And something within me felt conflicted.

Some months later, in a Victoria's Secret store in San Antonio, Texas, waiting for a friend to purchase some items, I watched and listened to two young ladies, both in their twenties, both rather plump and tattooed, as they shopped. They strolled around the display of frilly underwear, casually picking up one item, feeling its texture and dropping it back on the counter. Occasionally an Oooh or an Aaaah, an exclamation of appreciation. Then one of them picked up a particularly skimpy example and sought her friend's approval:

"Isn't this the sexiest thing you've ever seen?" she asked.

"For sure, and I love the little flowers on the front."

"But it costs $24.95. What do you think? I'm probably never going to use it."

"Oh come on", replied the friend "Its not about how often you use it. What's important is the minute before it comes off."

"The minute before it comes off." I thought. "That's what all that iron ore extraction is for."

A Fable

I am sitting in a forest of vast Oyamel trees, in the hills behind Valle de Bravo, Mexico. Each year, in November, tens of millions of monarch butterflies migrate from the northeast coast of the United States to this part of central Mexico to spend the winter. My six year-old granddaughter, Nuala, is with me. We have hiked up from the road for about an hour. The path winds up the steep hillside, crossing streams and opening occasionally to splendid views of the valley below. It is still early morning, the sun barely cutting through the thick leafy canopy of these Oyamel, a kind of fir tree. Above us, in the leaves, rest over a million monarch butterflies, their wings closed, hanging in clumps on the branches of the trees. On some branches there are so many butterflies that the branches bend, and appear to be the reddish brown of maples in Maine in September. They hang not only to the branches, but to each other, creating layers of hanging butterflies, all resting, wings closed, waiting for the sun to shine, to warm their wings, and urge them on their way to the stream in the skirts of the hills.

Nuala leans close to my ear: "Granpa, when are they going to move?" She recognises the sanctity of the place. There are other groups there, but no one speaks above a whisper, respecting the silence of the monarchs.

"Where do they all come from, Granpa?" she asks, her curiosity getting the better of her.

"Well, Nuala, it's like this:

Long ago, before even the times of the great human explorers like Marco Polo and Christopher Columbus, the creatures of our planet were exploring and adventuring. They explored to find new places to eat, to find warmer or colder climates, and, of course, for adventure. Creatures of the air, like the Artic Tern that flies from the Arctic to the Antarctic every year; Creatures of the land, like the wildebeest who gallops across the plains of the Serengeti twice a year, avoiding crocodiles as he crosses the Mara River and dodging hungry lions as he races through the savannah; and largest of all, Creatures of the sea, like the Humpback whale that swims from Alaska all the way to the bays of Baja California in Mexico, there to give birth to their baby whales.

"And butterflies, Granpa, do they explore?"

Oh yes, Dearly Beloved. Butterflies and other kinds of insects. This is the story of how Danaus plexixppus plexippus, a tiny insect, became the greatest explorer of all the insects in the world; he became King of the Butterflies. The thing about butterflies is that they are naturally explorers. They start their lives as caterpillars, wandering around the woods and gardens creeping along on their stomachs with their tiny hands and feet below them, eating leaves and plants. But, this gets boring, and so, at a certain point, oh Dearly Beloved, they wrap themselves up in a cocoon and sleep. And while they sleep they grow wings until, one fine sunny day, they eat their way out of the cocoon, spread their wings and begin to float on the breeze.

Danaus plexippus plexippus was a most 'mbishus[q] butterfly who was always adventuring farther. He lived in the deep, green woods of Canada, near the great Atlantic Ocean. In summertime, life was deliciously peaceful. He could spread his wings and the sun would warm

---

q Ambitious

them, and the breeze would lift them, and he would float from hill to hill. But in the winter it was horribly cold. The snow would fall on his wings and make them heavy. His favorite foods, which were various kinds of flowers, did not grow, and he was always hungry and cold.

One autumn it was terribly cold and the wisest old butterflies said it reminded them of the ice age when their lands froze and many, many butterflies died. That's when Danaus plexippus plexippus decided he would be a great explorer and would find the land where his family could spend the winter.

So, taking a group of his best friends and followers, Danaus plexippus plexippus set off from Canada. He flew South over the hills and lakes of Massachusetts. He flew West over the Great Mississippi River. He flew South over the Gulf of Mexico. And he kept on flying southwest until he reached the beautiful forests of Michoacán. Here, beside a village called Angangueo, he arrived one late October evening and saw hundreds of humans paddling their canoes into the middle of a lake, holding lighted candles and singing songs to their ancestors. It was the night of Dia de los Muertos, and as Danaus plexippus plexippus and his followers arrived, many of the humans believed that the butterflies were the returning souls of the humans' dead ancestors. Exhausted from their journey, the butterflies rested on the prows of the canoes and were welcomed by the humans who showed Danaus plexippus plexippus and his followers a forest of giant oyamel fir trees where they could make their home for the winter. Each morning as the sun rose, they spread their wings and felt the wondrous warmth of the day. They were happy. And they knew that this would be their winter home.

But something else miraculous happened too. When Danaus had lived in Canada, he and his family of butterflies had been colored a dull brown with specks of yellow. But as they warmed their wings each day, and as the sun shone on them, their colors grew more brilliant. By February, when they decided to return to Canada, their wings had become a brilliant array of brown and orange and yellow, with fine black lines marking them as special butterflies.

When they returned to Canada, Danaus plexippus plexippus and his followers found that many of their family had perished in the great freeze. So Danaus plexippus plexippus called a meeting of all the butterflies. He told them how the humans in Michoacán respected them, how tall and close to the sun are the oyamel fir trees, and how the butterflies should fly all the way to Mexico each year to grow strong and beautiful. All the butterflies admired the brilliant colored wings and happy tales of Danaus plexippus plexippus and his followers. They gave Danaus plexippus plexippus a special sash, like those you see on Presidents and Emperors, colored black with white spots, that Danaus plexippus plexippus wrapped around the tips of his wings, and they crowned him King of the Butterflies, which is why, today, he is called the Monarch.

Nuala sits looking up at the trees, the clumps of butterflies hanging together, and the shafts of light.

"Hush Granpa." She raises her index finger to her lips. "Can you hear that? It's like rain falling."

From above us there is a rustling. Like the reflections of light from the silver skin of blennies in a tide pool, like the shimmering of aspen leaves on a Colorado summer's day, the blades of light blur, shadows flit across the path, and there is a feeling of a breeze, but no air moves. First one, then ten, then one hundred butterflies disconnect from the pod, spread their wings and start to glide down the face of the hill toward the water. Many float down to us, alighting on our hands and heads. Soon, as they begin to move by the thousands, the noise of rustling leaves, the soft sound of a light rain, takes on a shape of its own, a shape derived from the wings of the butterflies beating against the air.

A snatch of verse occurs to me, and I recite it quietly:

Beside the lake, beneath the trees,
Fluttering and dancing in the breeze.

"What's that Granpa?"

"Oh, just a poem your grandmother used to recite. About daffodils, but it could just as well be about these butterflies."

We listen in amazed silence to the Sound of Butterflies.

ENDNOTES

1. **General Erskine:** General Erskine was descended from a long line of illustrious servants of Queen and Country. His grandfather, the Earl of Cromer, was Governor of Egypt, and, in 1908, in The Edinburg Review, published an article entitled "The Government of Subject Races" in which he stated:

> "Relations with whatsoever races are brought under [our] control must be politically and economically sound and morally defensible. . . . If we once have to draw the sword, not merely to suppress some local effervescence, but to overcome a general upheaval of subject races goaded to action either by deliberate oppression, ...or by unintentional misgovernment, ... the sword will assuredly be powerless to defend us for long, and the days of our Imperial rule will be numbered."

Unfortunately, grandson Erskine failed to follow the wisdom of his grandfather's words.

2. **Sir Barclay Nihill**

Although the appeal in Kenyatta v. Regina may not have exhibited the traits for which I so admired my grandfather, as I have researched I have repeatedly found examples of how he took a stand, often an unpopular stand, for those who have no rights. During the same period as the Kenyatta trial, Chief Koinange, one of the leaders of the KAU, was arrested and tried on a trumped up charge relating to the death of Chief Warahui. Dingle Foot, a prominent British barrister, later to become a Member of Parliament, was lead counsel. Mr. Foot was a strong advocate of British responsibility and fair play in its colonies, and represented numerous African and Indian causes celèbres during his career. Mr. Foot and Barclay were introduced socially, quickly developed a mutual respect, and often dined together. One evening Mr. Foot called on Barclay and asked if he could bring over a Mr. Desai who, according to the rumors on the street, was about to be arrested for subversive activities. Desai was an Indian activist for a multiracial society. He was close to the KAU and often acted as the KAU's informal lobbyist both in India and in Britain. Foot wanted Barclay to meet the man and, if appropriate, to intervene before the Government made any rash moves. Barclay agreed, provided that he could also invite John Wyatt, the Attorney General, A.G. Somerhough, the Deputy Public Prosecutor, and Anglican Archbishop Mathews. The following is an extract of an account of the meeting by Mr. Desai himself:

Seated on a wooden bench in the corner of Sir Nihill's home, I addressed my white audience as follows: 'I am a follower of Mahatma Gandhi and a believer in non-violence. I mean no harm to any Englishman. I have a large circle of Englishmen as my friends. But Africans need my help and I shall continue to help them. If you want to arrest me, you are most welcome to do so.' Sir Nihill then stood up shouting at the top of his voice: 'Well gentlemen, we shall not be influenced by the rumours that are being spread outside. But we shall be guided by what evidence we have in the court of law.' The meeting was over and the threat of potential arrest was thwarted.

Later, in 1955, Governor Baring appointed a Justice Holmes to prepare a report about alleged abuses at a court in Karatina and other administrative courts. The report was essentially a white wash, Governor Baring being of the school of white administrators who believed that the English rulers in Kenya could do no wrong. The matter reached the House of Commons in London, where one member demanded publication of the portions that mostly exonerated the administration. As Chief Justice of the East African Court of Appeals, Barclay Nihill, joined by the other judges, insisted that if there was selective disclosure of segments favorable to the administration, they would make public the rest of the report and would advocate for hearings into the abuses by the administration. No part of the report was published.

3. **Sir Richard Francis Burton**

As a child, Burton was raised in France and Italy, and spoke both languages fluently. He also spoke some Spanish, Portuguese and German, languages that he would later hone as he spent time in Brazil, the Portuguese island of Fernando Po, and in southern Germany. At Oxford he read Latin and Greek, but boring of their tediousness, found a professor who tutored him privately in Arabic and introduced him to various exotic aspects of the Kabbalah and the occult arts practiced by the Ismaili sect.

Upon leaving Oxford, Burton set off to India in the service of the Queen. Unlike most of his contemporaries in the British Army, who enjoyed India from afar....polo, gin & tonics, wives sent out from England...... Burton dived in to India, relished its smells, its customs, its strange, exotic peoples. His swarthy, almost gypsy complexion, and his black hair, which he let grow long, permitted him to pass as an Indian. He rapidly learned Hindustani, Gujurati and Persian, graduating in first place in each of these languages in the army language courses. Soon, the army was using him as a scout, or a kind of advance spy as they entered hostile territory. In the 1840s, also while in India, he was assigned to the court of the Prince Imam Agha Khan Makallati, the first Ismaili leader to take the name of Agha Khan, and the ancestor of the Aga Khan who played such a prominent role during our stay in Tanganyika. While at this court, Burton studied, and mastered, Sanskrit. During his travels around India he also picked up Sindhi, Marathi, Punjabi and two south Indian languages, Teluga and Toda.

After leaving his post in India, and embarking on his life as one of the most famous explorers of Eastern Africa, along with Livingstone and Speke, he learned Somali and Kiswahili from the east coast, and Kru and Mpingwa from the west. Finally, when posted to Brazil, he studied and wrote extensively about the Guarani, those warlike, but primitive people featured in the film, The Mission.

Burton's study of language led him to religious and sacred texts in many of the languages, and often, as he immersed himself in a language he also delved deep into their religion. His studies with his Hindu teacher, Him Chand, led Chand and the Nagar Brahma elders to accept Burton, in a weeklong ceremony of fasting and rituals, into their gotra, or caste of snake priests, an extraordinary feat given that movement upward through the Hindu caste system typically took several generations and reincarnations. He also studied and participated in the Tantric yoga practices, which, in their most profound form, indulged in religious/sexual acts of complex symbolism and ritual.

Possibly the religion with which Burton became most involved, and learned, was Islam. In the late 1840's Burton was posted to the Sind, in what is now the southwest corner of Pakistan. Here Sufism, a branch of Islam, permeated all aspects of life, and Burton, as always, dove in the deep end. He learned about a quarter of the Koran by heart and became a member of the Qadiri brotherhood of Sufism. He underwent the chillá, or forty-day fast, practiced meditation and the constant repetition of sacred words and phrases. After several years of study, Burton was admitted as a murshid, a holy wanderer, a man devoted to the religious life. He then took his immersion a step further. He joined that obscure and exotic group, the dervishes. These men practiced an ancient ritual of prayer and chanting, reaching a state of ecstasy in which they whirled in circles brandishing spears, often cutting themselves and others in the process. Burton engaged fully, suffering the cuts and gashes of the ecstatically transformed, all in his search for the most intense religious experience.

During this period Burton became obsessed with the idea that he should visit Mecca, the holy city of Islam. This was perilous for two reasons. First, being Burton, in order to secure funds from the Royal Geographical Society, he wanted to start in Muscat, on the easternmost tip of the Arabian peninsular, and trek westward across the heretofor uncharted desert. Second, while the pilgrimage to Mecca, or the haj, is required of every able bodied practicing Muslim, at least once in his or her life, the sacred city is also very closely guarded from, and prohibited to, non-Muslims. If he should be discovered not to be a Muslim, and given the era, that probably meant discovered to be a European even though he had studied Islam devoutly, he would probably be killed.

Posing as a Sunni Darwaysh, a blessed vagabond and member of the Mystic Path, or tariqa, Burton let his hair grow long, applied kohl to his eyes, and for a month before embarking on the pilgrimage, lived in one of the poorer sections of Cairo, acclimatizing himself and reacquainting himself with all the little details of accent, hand movements, sacred references, etc. that could give him away or aid in his disguise. Needless to say, Burton entered the Holy City, wrote copious notes on tiny scraps of paper – so as to avoid being noticed and placed under suspicion - drew sketches of the Mosque, and numerous drawings of street life in Mecca.

Not content with travelling to Mecca, to remotest Kashmir and the mountains of Afghanistan, Burton also set out to discover the source of the Nile. With a team of African porters, and a mountain of scientific instruments he set out from Kaole, some 5 kilometers south of Bagamoyo and travelled over 7 months to reach Lake Tanganyika. This was not the source of the Nile, and Burton was not to be part of the expedition, led by Speke, that actually found the source of the Nile, at the northern end of Lake Victoria in August 1858. He was repeatedly struck down by malaria and often had to be carried, delirious, by his men. During the course of this journey he learned various African languages, and studied the flora and fauna of eastern Africa, reporting on it in exhausting detail.

Throughout all this exploring and adventuring, Burton read and wrote endlessly. He was inclined to poetry and was the first man to translate, possibly the first Englishman to read, the Kama Sutra.

4. **The African Nationalist Movement**

The origins of the turbulence go back generations, but the Second World War was the initial catalyst for change. As the European powers coalesced to fight the Nazi threat, the colonial powers – Britain, France, and Belgium – looked to their colonies for support. The argument was that the world would be a better place free of Nazi rule. The colonies sent their men in large numbers. Not just whites, but Africans too. They took heart in the words of the Atlantic Charter, an accord reached by Britain and the United States in 1941, which declared all peoples' right to self-determination. And then, after the war, they were further encouraged by the independence of India and Pakistan in 1947.

After the war, and especially in the early '50s, African Nationalist movements sprouted throughout Africa. Some of the leaders of the movement, men like Kwame Nkrumah in Ghana, Julius Nyerere in Tanganyika, Kenneth Kaunda in Northern Rhodesia, later Zambia, and Dr. Hastings Banda in Nyasaland, later Malawi, were scholars, peaceful men who sought peaceful means to a peaceful end, men who saw the success achieved by Mahatma Gandhi and Nehru in India. Others, like those in Uganda and Kenya, were lead by men who carried the mantle of authority (the leader of the Ugandan movement was Kabaka Mutesa II, King of the Baganda people; Kenyatta was chosen by his Kikuyu peers, and supported by other tribes who recognized his gravitas and leadership) and who, while advocating peaceful means were not above turning a blind eye to the activities of more violent activists. And yet others, especially in the Belgian and Portuguese colonies, were lead by opportunists, men who might today be called Freedom Fighters or even terrorists.

5.   **The British Response to African Nationalism**

The British claimed to walk a more moderated and rational path to freedom for their colonies in sub-Saharan Africa than did their French and Belgian counterparts. With hindsight, it is arguable that the speed at which Britain granted independence to its African colonies was in direct and inverse relation to the number and influence of British settlers within the colony. Ghana was the first to go, in 1957. Then Nigeria in 1960. Neither had a British settler community. Tanganyika was next in 1961, and Uganda in 1962. Neither of these had a significant settler community. But Britain had no interest in letting go of Kenya, with over 55,000 whites, Rhodesia, with some 250,000 whites, and South Africa with an even larger population of both British and Dutch origin white settlers.

6.   **French, Belgian and Portuguese Reaction To African Nationalism**

The four major colonial powers reacted to this Nationalist movement in different ways. The French had suffered devastating defeats in two of their colonies in the 50's: Vietnam, which fell to the Vietnamese in the Battle of Dien Bien Phu in 1954; and Algeria, from which the French withdrew in 1962 after 8 years of fighting. Some 900,000 Frenchmen returned to France from Algeria, shattering the French psyche and traumatizing their view of colonial Africa. In the course of 11 months during 1960, the French granted independence to 14 colonies in Africa. In sub Saharan Africa, only tiny Djibouti, on the Somali coast, remained French after 1960. Clearly, the timetable for Independence was in no way based on these colonies' preparedness for self-rule. It was purely a function of the French abdication of their responsibilities and a retrenchment into internal (and EU) politics.

The Belgians, frankly, had no business being in Africa. While they had colonies - The Congo, Rwanda and Burundi - they had no colonial infrastructure, no vision of their role in Africa. They left the management of their colonies to a handful of corporate enterprises whose main goal was to deplete the colonies of their natural resources as quickly and as cost effectively as possible. The Congo, Belgium's largest colony, was effectively controlled by La Societé General de Belgique, through its subsidiary Compagnie du Congo pour le Commerce et l'Industrie, and by La Force Publique, a brutal military force led entirely by Belgian officers. They made no effort to educate the local population beyond primary level. Indeed, university education was forbidden to Africans until 1955. Education was placed in the hands of missionaries, primarily Catholic missionaries who viewed the role of their education system as the training of priests for proselytizing and converting Congolese pagans. At the time of independence, only 16 Congolese (from a population of 13 million) had graduated university. The Belgians viewed the colony as primarily a source of cheap natural resources.

When the Belgians saw the French pulling out, they too rushed for the exit. On June 30, 1960, the Belgian Congo was granted its independence. However, at the time of independence, there was a complete void in the areas of law, civil engineering, medicine and in the military and political skills needed to run a country. No Congolese had risen beyond the ranks of non-commissioned officer in the Force Publique. The formal education of the first Prime Minister of the newly independent country, Patrice Lumumba, was a mission school followed by a one-year post office training program. It was consequently no surprise when, only weeks after the Belgian Congo attained its independence, there was a revolt among the African soldiers of the Force Publique, and the province of Katanga seceded from the Congo, declaring itself an independent nation under the leadership of Moishe Tshombe, a business man closely linked with Belgian mining interests. Civil war ensued. Another revolt against the central government broke out in Kasai province leading to more bloodshed. On September 14, 1960, Prime Minister Lumumba was overthrown by Colonel Joseph Mobutu, and then murdered while in detention in Katanga, eight days before John F. Kennedy's inauguration. The Congo was a disaster and the United Nations forces moved in during 1961 to establish some semblance of calm. Some 80,000 Belgians fled the country, most of them through a Belgian government airlift in June 1961.

If the French and the Belgians were hands-off in the extreme, leaving their colonies in the disarray of tribal conflicts and incompetent leaders, the Portuguese presented the other end of the spectrum. In 1960, Portugal was under the dictatorial thumb of President Salazar. He would brook no resistance within his homeland, and he would brook even less in his colonies. Angola and Mozambique were the two primary Portuguese colonies, and Mozambique, like the Congo, shared a border with Tanganyika.

7. Julius Nyerere

Nyerere was the son of a local chieftain. He was educated first by missionaries and then attended Edinburg University in Scotland. He was soft-spoken, gentle and reserved. He had been selected to lead Tanganyika several years earlier, and carried himself with the air of an aristocratic literature professor. Tanganyika gained its Independence in 1961 with Nyerere as its first President.

He was one of the early proponents of what became known as African Socialism, a view of African development based in strengthening village life, rather than investing capital in development. He liked to be known as Mwalimu, or teacher. He spent heavily on education and within 10 years the literacy rate in Tanzania had risen from about 20% to nearly 90%. He described his brand of Socialism as Ujamaa, or "family hood". It was, he said, "opposed to capitalism, which seeks to build a happy society on the basis of the exploitation of man by man. And it is equally opposed to doctrinaire Socialism, which seeks to build its happy society on a philosophy of the inevitable conflict between man and man".

Although Nyerere himself admitted that he left the country in a worse financial condition than he found it, his regime was not an entire failure. Unlike many of the independent African states founded by his contemporaries, Tanzania was politically stable and firmly egalitarian. He left behind a population with one of the highest literacy rates in Africa. To my impressionable young mind, here was an African hero, a man who could change how the world saw Africa. His philosophy impacted me and sowed the seeds of a healthy skepticism for Western solutions for the third world. I always had a soft spot in my heart for Mwalimu, the Teacher. He was that rare specimen, a completely honest, completely committed, politician.

8. **Rock art in Ennedi: Hallucinogenic mushrooms**. Gérard Bailloud, with a group of researchers sponsored by *Musée de l'Homme* in Paris, spent a full

year inspecting, identifying and photographing some 155 sites in the Ennedi mountain range. Gérard Bailloud: *Art rupestre en Ennedi* (1997) (Looking for Rock Paintings and Engravings in the Ennedi Hills) is the result of this year of researching, and is the most comprehensive published work on the Ennedi rock paintings. The hallucinogenic mushrooms we found represented on the walls of our U shaped camp site are not mentioned in the book.